A Leap of Faith

Going, doing and changing ourselves
and the world around us

A Leap of Faith

We are here

Going, doing and changing ourselves and the world around us

David Bernard-Stevens

A Leap of Faith
Going, doing and changing ourselves
and the world around us

First published in 2015 by
Panoma Press Ltd
48 St Vincent Drive, St Albans, Herts, AL1 5SJ UK

info@panomapress.com
www.panomapress.com

Cover design by Michael Inns
Artwork by Karen Gladwell

ISBN 978-1-909623-97-2

The rights of David F. Bernard-Stevens to be identified as the author of this work has been asserted in accordance with sections 77 and 78 of the Copyright Designs and Patents Act 1988.

A CIP catalogue record for this book is available from the British Library.

All rights reserved. No part of this work may be reproduced in any material form (including photocopying or storing in any medium by electronic means and whether or not transiently or incidentally to some other use of this publication) without the written permission of the copyright holder except in accordance with the provisions of the Copyright, Designs and Patents Act 1988. Applications for the copyright holder's written permission to reproduce any part of this publication should be addressed to the publishers.

This book is available online and in all good bookstores.

Copyright © 2015 David F. Bernard-Stevens

Contents

Dedication — ix
Foreword — xi
Prologue — xv

October 31, 2013 — 1
An unsettled spirit
Being a phony and divorce
Genius
The mother of all lows
Family crisis

December 8, 2013 — 21
The need to think differently
Becoming a squirrel
Declaring to the universe and God
Losing my job
Hand-to-hand Global Leadership
Not seeing things clearly

December 24, 2013 — 39
Jamaica
The link to Kenya
Being broke and lost
The concept of the single step
The moment of knowing
A choice and a leap
The God within us
Learning to let go

January 22, 2014 — 59
Connecting to Gandhi
Mindsets, memories and reactions
Training the abused women of Kibera
Kibera... a life changer for them and me

February 2, 2014 — 85
How we create our realities
Mindsets, formations and twomations
A secret for communicating better
Reacting and repeating and prison
The magnitude of what we do not know
Using prevailing mindsets to control us
To change we must think differently

March 25, 2014 — 107
Understanding faith
Creating the win/win... all the time
Trying to control outcomes is nonsense
Coming home and making discoveries

April 1, 2014 — 123
Fighting my lows without medications
The importance of knowing one's purpose
Cameroon
Throwing out judgment in order to see clearly
Discovering the real Kenya

May 15, 2014 — 143
A history of the women brewers
Kenya's post-election violence
Being an object or a human being
Creating something from nothing
The choices that created something special
A choice that made a huge difference
Meeting Ruth
Learning to say no yet still seeing the starfish
Organizations – mindsets needing to evolve
The magical Africa and Kenya I began to see
The proposal
Negotiating for cows – blending two cultures

June 23, 2014   193
Core values and purpose
Curiosity , the trip inward and the God within
Why so many trainings have failed
What if we learned to think differently?
A problem – telling people what they should know
Why sustainability has not been achieved
The miracle of the dairy herd
Helping is not that simple
Conflict, stress and school fees
Attracting from a non-judgmental universe
Asking forgiveness

September 17, 2014   229
We are our thoughts – the need for reflection
Our journey, the joys and the fear
From death comes Life
A choice to find meaning and joy
The future is still to be written
Choosing to be all we were created to be

January, 2015 – Acknowledgements   241

About the Author   243

Testimonials   247

Dedication

I THOUGHT about all of the people who have been part of my life, and of course this book has been created from all of their inputs, advice, kicks in the pants when needed, as well as a helping hand when I fell down or became discouraged. I fell down a lot. They are all part of my learning whose wisdom can be found throughout these pages. They will forever be part of my heart.

But this dedication is to all those who find themselves full of doubt, fighting discouragement and despair, and who may have a sense that no matter what they attempt to do, the world will push them down further. And yet they still manage to take another step and survive another day.

This book and these letters are written with them firmly in my mind and heart. It is to them, along with my prayers, hopes and yes, guidance where I can, for each to realize there is hope. It is my fervent prayer that they find within these letters the way forward where, no matter what happens, each can find meaning and joy in every moment of every day. And in the end, what could be better than that?

Naturally, I also want to dedicate this work to my sons, David and Matt. They have met their struggles head on, sometimes falling but always getting up again to move forward. May you unleash that power I know is within you and do something special for the people and world around you. May you find peace and joy within your spirit each day no matter what the world throws your way. You have my admiration and love and I am proud to be your father... no matter what.

Foreword

ABOUT 10 YEARS ago I was lucky enough to be asked to write a book. If you haven't had that privilege I can tell you it feels like an explicit endorsement of who you are and what you represent but also offers up the frightening possibility of making an utter fool of yourself in public. You wonder what your friends and family and the people down your street will think of you when they read what you have to say. So maybe you choose to hold back, just a bit, and in that moment you lose - you lose the opportunity to connect with a real person who is in need of the inspiration, encouragement and support that only your words could have provided, if only you had had the courage to tell it like it is (or was).

We, all of us look, for validation, understanding, forgiveness and love. We share our stories, our dramas and our hope, dreams and fears with those closest to us in order to make sense of our lives and to reassure us of our choices. But deciding to write a book that is honest, truthful and heartfelt is not something anyone with even a modicum of common sense should take lightly.

So here's the thing, David has written something that is painfully honest. And the most remarkable thing for me is that it is about a "work in progress". There is no "sterilizing" gap between facing the challenge and reaching the goal. This isn't a book reflecting on some great but distant adventure but an ongoing journey that is still difficult and painful and unfolding.

I wish there were more books like it. Richard Branson once posed a question, "If Nelson Mandela had died sometime during his imprisonment on Robben Island and had never become the Leader and President of South Africa, what would we (the world) think of him?"

Branson's point was that becoming President wasn't what made Mandela, Mandela. Becoming President just made him more famous. All the qualities that made him who he was were there as he struggled during his 27 years in prison. They were there before his prison sentence and they were there after he was released.

Compared to Mandela few will have heard of DBS, I don't suppose this book will sell as many copies as *Long Walk to Freedom* and yet I feel sure Mandela would agree that that is a shame because this book does something very special, it sheds light on how it feels to put everything on the line to follow what one knows to be right even when few will ever know of or appreciate our efforts.

I've just about finished reading another book, collected thoughts and writings from the Spanish Civil War. Again it struck me how different it is to read about something that is "in the past" to something that is still on-going. If you are wondering what it feels like to be on the "front line" of a meaningful, rewarding and challenging life right now, at a time in life when most of us would be only too keen to retire and put their feet up, you owe it to yourself to read David's story, one I hope that will continue to unfold for many years to come. I defy anyone not to be inspired.

Andy Ferguson
Enseignant
Only One Intention
Edinburgh, Scotland

Prologue

THE WORLD is a mysterious place. It is a world within a chaotic universe where few things, if any, can be counted on to last and where no rational reason seems to exist for the things that happen. Good things happen to bad people and bad things can happen to the best of people who are doing all they can to make sense out of their lives. That includes me.

And yet amid all of the chaos there seems to be a set of rules that surrounds it all or at least the universe seems to embrace. They are as mysterious as the world and give up their secrets very slowly and begrudgingly. And yet they are out there as surely as gravity was out there prior to Mr. Newton becoming aware of its existence.

Most of us are just too engaged with surviving each day of life or the politics of the office to become aware of them… but sometimes there are modern day Newtons who seem to see more than most of us do. We need to pay more attention to what they are discovering as it truly can change the way we see the world. It can change the way we see ourselves.

For me it took a long time before I began to listen and learn from those paying more attention to things going on in the world around us. The more I learned, the more my world began to change. More precisely, the way I began to *experience* my life within the world changed. In time, like Newton, I began to see, feel, and experience things that had always been present but had remained hidden amid the chaotic rush of my everyday life.

I also began to understand the main reason for my blindness. I had been trapped within a mental prison of my own construction. I had been trapped within a world of my own making from all the bits of information my mind had stored and all the experiences I had endured up to that point. And as I began to become aware of my own personal prison, I came to understand a deeper sense that if I did not escape this prison, my experience of life would continue to be one with little meaning and sadly of far too little joy no matter what I accomplished.

So I began to listen more to those who, like Newton, were showing the way to a better way to live… a better way to experience life and what living truly could be. In time, I began to walk a different path where some amazing people and new experiences helped point the way and yes, pick me up when I fell down. I fell down a lot. I still do.

And though people have always encouraged me to write of my experiences and learning, I hesitated as I was still trying to figure things out myself. But now I think the time has come and I am ready to share... the good and the not so good parts of my life, my actions, the life I once lived and the life I have now created.

Yet HOW to tell the story was a quite a quandary. I was talking with a friend, Maria Carlton from Australia, a brilliant writer in her own right, when I saw the way forward. We were speaking about family and I mentioned the deep regrets I still harbor about not asking my late father questions about his life, dreams and the reasons behind the choices he made. It was at that moment I decided to share my story with the world while at the same time sharing it with my two sons who, if like me, would also have regrets upon my demise for not taking time to ask the questions to understand and know their father.

I am ready to tell you and them my story of what I did, why and more importantly, the learning that has come with my unpredictable and at times surprising journey. I hope the learning contained within my adventure will help you create a life of meaning, purpose and joy no matter what circumstances come your way, for it is truly within your power to do so.

As for my sons, David and Matt, I hope they choose to make their own prison break and see the things around them which have always been there but have remained hidden from their reality. I hope they, and you, will find within these letters the concepts needed to change your own life and by doing so, change the lives of others you will encounter every day... not by what you say, but by what you will do and most importantly WHY!

Each of us will create meaning for the experiences within our lives each day. Yet to create a life and reality that has purpose and can bring with it joy and fulfillment we must learn to think differently, understand that in each moment there are infinite possibilities and that we have the power within us to choose the kind of person we will become and the path we will eventually travel.

The how and why of all this is contained within the following letters...

October 31, **2013**

Dear David and Matt

Trying to explain my life and the choices I have made seems like trying to capture a cloud. The more I get my arms around it, the faster it slips through my fingers. It is like trying to remember a dream which was so clear at the moment of its conception but over time has become simply vague memories – bits of pieces if you will – individually making little sense. And yet somewhere within all those bits and pieces the answers for my life exist along with the reason for my existence.

For the past few years I have diligently worked, painfully at times, to put those pieces together to find something that made sense to me about life in general. As you are my only two sons, I want to share with you what I have found so you may someday understand the "whys" of your father's life. I wish to do this because if you are like me (and both of you are in so many ways) you will one day wish you had taken time to ask me these things and not let time slip away as it did with my father and me.

I remember being with my father as he lay dying in his hospital bed. We had drifted apart during the last 15 years or so of his life. We both hated that. Neither of us wanted it but seemed powerless to adjust to what was happening. For my part I just didn't know how to change the way my life was unfolding. I seemed to be at the mercy of the shifting winds upon a raging sea, looking anywhere and everywhere for a lifeline just to stay afloat.

In the end, we made our peace, said what needed to be said and were together once more. But there was not enough time for my questions or his answers.

In looking back, there were so many times I wish I had asked him what he thought about certain things or more importantly why he chose to do what he did. Perhaps most of all I wish I could have heard from his own point of view what really happened in his life and where he was trying to go. So for me, the real essence of his life will forever be a mystery, which is sad as he was a unique spirit I think.

So it is with this in mind I write these open letters to the two of you and others who may be looking to find their own ways to discover meaning for their lives. I do not know if you or others will ever read these letters, but if you are ever curious, many of the answers to your unasked questions will be here. And perhaps, as my journey is revealed, you may discover the tools to find and travel the journey each of you was created to travel.

You are both such amazing paradoxes where in many ways you are both so much alike and yet so different. And though the circumstances of your lives have formed the basis for your choice not to share much of your lives with each other, you should know that each of you has a deep spirit of wanting to serve others and the loving characteristics of caring, respect and empathy for humanity. I know you will find your own ways of making a difference to those you encounter. My hope is you will eventually choose to share your gifts with each other and with those closest to you as you age and grow in wisdom.

Let me start with what might be on your minds most... what happened that took me away from you and my life in Nebraska to come and live in Kenya? How, and perhaps more importantly why, did the person you knew as Dad the teacher, the Senator, the President of a Chamber of Commerce become divorced from your mother, move to a country in Africa, marry an African woman from the Kalenjin tribe of Kenya and begin what must look like a totally different life separated and apart from you? More to the point, "What the heck happened and why?!"

So with a deep breath, let me begin my story there.

My spirit was always unsettled... always. It may not have seemed that way to you or to others but inside I was usually conflicted. I do not understand it all yet but there was always a sense of something more I should be doing and whatever I was doing was never it.

The pattern started in full when I was a teacher soon after I was chosen as one of four national finalists for Teacher of the Year in the United States. And though I loved teaching, there came a point when teaching simply could not calm that feeling in the pit of my stomach telling me I was supposed to be doing something else... something bigger. So I began to search elsewhere.

Then quite by accident I was chosen to be a State Senator by Kay Orr who was the first woman governor of the State of Nebraska. My appointment was a shock to most, including your mother, particularly since I had neither applied nor desired it. Those in the political "know" believed I would lose my first special election as I was a political unknown with little political party background or support. And yet I surprised them all by never losing an election until I chose to walk away from it all mid-term during my ninth year.

One of the reasons I stated for stepping down from being a Senator was the desire to spend more time with family. This was true as the political conflicts and at times hostile behaviors people exhibited toward both your mother and me had taken its toll. For reasons I will speak of later, people say and do things to politicians they would *never* do to another human being. Even the two of you were threatened. We kept that from you of course, even as the police took extra precautions in monitoring our home. Your mother was never one to deal with conflict well and unfortunately for her I was usually found in the midst of the more meaningful and controversial political fights.

There were, however, other reasons I resigned my Senate seat I did not speak of at the time: one, my spirit was telling me I was turning into someone I should not be and two, I knew there was something else I should be doing even though I knew not what. There was always that feeling in the pit of my stomach telling me I was not doing what I was meant to do.

Like I stated in the beginning, my spirit had never been at peace for as long as I can remember.

So I became President of the local Chamber of Commerce and it was there things began to totally unravel which incredibly impacted the two of you I suspect. For the record, I did not want to take that job. I wanted to take a year off to find the path to the future I had been searching for, but the pressures of the expectations of others proved more than I could withstand. Reluctantly, I took the job.

Being President of a community Chamber of Commerce was all very straightforward. All I needed to do was stroke the egos of those having positions of authority (bank presidents, mayors, wealthy business people, city council members etc.), convince the chamber membership that their membership fees were valuable for the growth of the community, run an efficient staff and all would be good until retirement. Unfortunately for me, I just could not buy into it. There was no meaning there for me.

Quite simply, I really disliked that job and I felt like a phony... and in a very real way I was. I was playing the role I thought a Chamber President was expected to play on a community stage and it was a role not suited for who I was or needed to be. I was miserable. I was truly an actor upon the world's stage playing whatever role presented itself, never getting to play the role I was given at birth – the role of simply being David. Too many people in the world are on a similar stage playing roles meant for someone else I think.

As for your mother and me, we tried very hard to keep things together during this time but we were unable to find ways of overcoming the negative effects on our relationship from my being a Senator. Combined with my daily misery at work this continued to be a very difficult time for your mother and me. Over time we decided that divorce was in our best interests and hopefully the two of you would understand.

To this day I really do not know what the two of you felt although if you were like me when my parents divorced, there was a huge sense of loss in terms of my home and the sense of security I had felt. All of that simply vanished overnight. And though I understood it in terms of my parents' happiness, for me nothing was ever the same. Perhaps your experiences were similar.

Thus began a most difficult part of my life and I suspect yours. It was determined by specialists I was, and had been for many years, suffering from depression and there was a strong sense I was what professionals referred to as "borderline hypo bipolar." Surprisingly I found some comfort in this as it put a face on the huge mood swings I had experienced for most of my life. Where prior to knowing I just assumed this was what life was supposed to feel like, I now knew there were reasons why I felt the way I did and I began to understand my own behaviors more.

To give you a sense of the mood swings, when I was on a "high cycle" I could do amazing things and life was wonderful. Yet when I was in a "low cycle" everything became much harder. I could still think well, mind you, but it took much more energy and concentration to do so. The world was also much "darker" during the low cycles as compared to the warm bask of the sun experienced during the highs.

I wish I could find the words to describe my high and low experiences. The truth is, at times during my highs I could be brilliant, particularly on connecting the dots from one concept to other more abstract ones. I remember once I was in a group discussion and though I had only briefly scanned the book being discussed there came a point where I challenged one of the points made by the minister leading the discussion saying, "But isn't the point you just made going against the basic premise the author makes at the end of the book?" The minister agreed but asked that I be patient as the group was not "there" yet.

On the way home I was verbally assaulted by someone who knew I had barely scanned the book an hour or so prior to the class. I remember them asking why I pretended to be so smart by stating I knew something of the author's opinion at the end when I had not even thoroughly read the book!

I do not remember how I actually responded, but it went something like, "One doesn't have to read the book to get a sense of what the author is trying to say." This led to the person saying in exasperation, "OK Mr. Smarty-Pants, you think you are so smart, let's have you take one of those computer intelligence tests when we get home. Let's see once and for all how smart you really are!"

Now I knew I was feeling pretty good and when on a high I can always sense things, even knowing sometimes what was going to happen. Don't ask how. I don't know how, I just know what is going to happen. So they picked a test for me to take, one of those 20 question timed things. I did it and pushed finished. The results were such that the person never brought up the topic again. It came back "genius." I am not saying that I am a genius, what I am saying is that when I am on a high cycle, my mind works extremely well.

The lows are another story as so many in the world who experience similar things can readily attest. Like the highs, the lows vary in intensity. At their worst... well let me give you a sense of what it feels like by sharing a real experience.

When in the midst of a low cycle it was (and is) as if I am on the edge of a cliff overlooking a huge bottomless pitch-black pit. My struggle to keep things together could be likened to there being forces trying to push me into that abyss with me constantly struggling just to keep from falling. The struggle never seemed to stop and to fall would be the end for there was no bottom to this pit. It was dark, lonely and as close to what hell might be as I care to get.

The energy needed to keep from falling was huge... a point perhaps only those who suffer from depression can fully comprehend. My mind was still pretty good, but to think was much harder and those things that before came so easily were not nearly so easy anymore. I had little patience, fought to be civil and worked hard to keep a simmering frustration and anger from boiling over. Having said all of that, it was during a low that my life changed forever.

I was in the Middle East, Tel Aviv to be specific, when "The Mother of All Lows" made her appearance. I was there to do a leadership program and a guest of a wonderful person I had met through a leadership program. I had just returned to Tel Aviv from Jerusalem and the West Bank and we were designing our upcoming workshop. All of a sudden I knew I had to stop as I was clearly sensing an oncoming "low."

I had always been able to at least function during a low, but this one felt different. It seemed stronger and more powerful than anything I had experienced before and I knew I needed to lie down. It was mid-evening and I politely stopped our planning session and went to bed stating I was not feeling well, which was accurate. But something was very wrong and very different this time. I could sense it. I could feel it.

I know what I am about to say will sound strange yet it is what I experienced whether true or imaginary, of which sometimes there can be such a fine line separating the two.

I was lying on the guestroom bed and out on that cliff's edge again. But this time there were more forces trying to push me over the edge and I was having the fight of my life to keep from falling. And then it happened. I was pushed off and I was gone... falling into the abyss. I was shocked as I had never fallen before. My mind tried to come to my rescue and I remember thinking: David you are not falling, just put your hand down on the floor... see? You are on a bed and not falling. You are fine.

But I knew I wasn't fine. It was as if my body was in the bed but I, meaning my spirit, was falling and if help did not come soon my spirit was going to die. I was falling and I could not stop it no matter how hard I tried to come to grips with what my spirit was feeling.

I had met someone about a year earlier where at the time of our first meeting it seemed we had known each other for a very long time. Over time we developed a good friendship. So as I was lying on the bed I opened my laptop, got online and typed in a message to her out of pure desperation, "Please help! I'm falling!"

To my instant relief she was there. She gave me a phrase to say which I shall never forget, "God will give me perfect peace because my mind stays upon him." She told me to say it over and over again and that help would come. I trusted her more than anyone in the world at that point so I let go of my sense of despair of falling and just concentrated on saying that phrase over and over again.

Slowly I sensed my fall slowing and eventually I came to a full stop. But I was not coming back up. I was just floating in some sort of limbo unable to see the light from above and sensing the deep darkness of the abyss below.

After a period of time she asked if I sensed anything around me. After taking note about where I was, I suddenly sensed, perhaps felt, an energy source behind me and two toward my feet. She told me they were angels who were there to protect me and to not despair but to hold on. I had not believed in things like angels before, yet now I sensed energy around me and I *did* feel safe in the sense I was not going to fall anymore. I believed her.

But how to get back up? I was simply unable to move upward no matter how hard I tried within my spirit and mind to do so. Was this it? Was this where I was going to be spiritually the rest of my life, somewhere trapped between the light above and the dark abyss below?

I typed the message to my trusted lifeline-holding friend that I was OK but I was unable to come back. She told me to hold on as her "spirit man" was coming. In a few moments she asked me to look for it above and I felt, sensed... I don't know... but there was a huge arm and powerful hand reaching down for me. I grabbed hold of that hand and slowly her spirit man pulled me up and back into the light.

She then told me I was safe now. She added the angels would remain to protect me but I needed to sleep now as all was OK and she would check back with me in the morning. I slept truly the sleep of peace in the waning hours of that night.

Now here is the final part of that experience which still gives me goosebumps whenever I think about it.

The next time she and I spoke about that night she informed me of two things: first, that just before I sent my first Skype message she was not near her computer. She said somehow she got the feeling she should check and that I might be in need of help. That is why she was there when I typed my first cry for help. Second, my friend who is very strong in her Christian faith told me after she knew I had fallen she had been talking with God in prayer. That is how she knew the angels were coming to help and later to protect.

But when I was unable to come up into the light she prayed for God to help me. She told me it was God who told her to send her spirit man to help me. When she protested saying that she was not worthy to do something he could do, he simply laughed and said, "David does not believe in me enough yet for me to help… but he believes in you and as such you can bring him back into the light. It's OK he is learning, but don't delay."

I know how strange this story might seem to you and to others, yet I know what I experienced and felt. And I know what the Skype messages said.

I can also say I have never had a low like that ever again and won't either for I know what to say and do to stay within the light. Surprisingly, besides repeating the phrase I also must "let go" in order not to fall. Sometimes one has to allow others to help even if they are angels and/or God, Allah, Yahweh or the Great Spirit. But if they are to help, one needs to let go of trying to control all things.

In other words, the harder I struggled, the more difficult things became. Once I let go and had faith I would not fall, all was calm and there was no fear. This lesson would continue to develop and mature the more my life continued to change. It was here where my self-leadership journey collided with another path or journey, this one being spiritual. It was the eventual merging of these two paths that would develop a truer sense of what real leadership needed to be both in my life and in the world.

My lows still come and sometimes they are tough yet I now know everything will pass and the light will always overtake the darkness. And with that the darkness lost its control over me. Your dad is not afraid of the dark of the abyss anymore. I respect it for it is there but I am not afraid.

I know that was a jump to a later part of my story to you, yet I thought it important that you realize the internal struggles I seemed to be enduring throughout my life.

But let me get back to my story and my playing the role of being the President of the North Platte, Nebraska Area Chamber of Commerce.

At the time of being the Chamber's President, I knew nothing of how to deal with my lows and when the challenges of those combined with the emotions coming from the divorce process, I was a bit overwhelmed at times... and the times were about to get worse.

If it sounds like I believed I was a victim it is because that is exactly what I believed. Poor me. Poor poor me...

As both of you know, besides the divorce, we had a family issue arise that had a profound effect on almost all of us. This crisis would begin to change everything including the stage upon which I had been role-playing most of my life. That stage was about to shift dramatically to the point where I would have to choose whether to continue pretending to be what I thought I needed to be or to be who I was created to be. It was the classic "to be or not to be" question!

As I stated earlier, I was a pretender and a good one at that! I knew what a Senator was supposed to be and look like so I played that role. I knew what a President of a Chamber should be like and I played that role too. Yet through the course of our family's challenges I began to understand more of who I really was and the degree of pretending I had done throughout my life. As I grew in my understanding and awareness, I began to change.

It's ironic how a crisis for another within our family turned out to be such a turning point for me. Thomas Jefferson was fond of saying "... a little rebellion now and then is a good thing and as necessary in the political world as storms in the physical." Perhaps that applies to personal storms as well.

In fact for me, over the course of the next few years everything would change. The groundwork was being laid for my eventual going away from you and the life I knew but for now I was still unaware of what was to come.

As you both know, the entire family came together which is what good families do when facing a crisis. If you recall, your mother and her new husband, the two of you and I along with my "significant other" at the time all went to workshops and seminars that would in the end help keep things together.

For me, two families having suffered and anguished much during the divorce and eventual splitting apart, yet finding a way to come together again as one for the love of another is something not often found in my experience. As dysfunctional as we may have been, we overcame it when it was needed most. That is something truly remarkable.

My personal experiences in those trainings that took place in Chicago were life changing. They opened my eyes to what life could be. People began teaching and leading me along a path I never knew existed. In time that path led me to discovering who I truly was and what I was meant to do... the purpose I had always sensed but could never find.

My life was beginning to change both within and without. It was filled with confusion, excitement, joy, fear, curiosity, sadness and every other emotion one might imagine when all one knows is being transformed. I was the caterpillar experiencing its transformation into something totally different, and like the caterpillar I had no idea what was happening and was powerless to stop it.

I was finally becoming aware of who I had been (a pretender) and more importantly that I had it within me to change to what my spirit knew I needed to be. However, knowing I had the power and learning how to use it to change the reality of my life would become a long and ongoing process.

So let me end this letter by saying to you that it was here, in the turmoil of a family crisis and the changes going on within my spirit and mind where I found the beginning constructs of my core values or those things which my spirit needed in order to thrive. They were the things that I would fight for when push came to shove.

I began to recognize the value these concepts had upon me above all others: respect, transparency, curiosity, humor, integrity, accountability, inclusiveness and speaking one's truth. And though there was much still to learn, I finally understood that when I aligned my thoughts, choices and actions with those core values I was able to fly, life began to have meaning and I felt a deeper experience of joy.

I began to realize my purpose which included serving others and teaching those seeking to learn what I was beginning to understand about self-leadership and the concepts of how to think differently in order to create a life of meaning and joy. I also sensed I would not be playing small anymore in terms of what I wanted to create. That, and a knowing I would soon enter the world stage to help make a difference for people began forming the foundations for the new reality I would eventually create. I did not know where, how or what my future was going to look like but I knew this was the path I was meant to travel. I was terrified and excited all at the same time.

This is what began my journey to a world totally foreign to my experience. This is where my personal leadership journey of becoming who I was created to be truly began. It is where I began to understand, even after being a Senator, you cannot lead anyone until first learning to lead yourself. I also began to understand the huge difference between having a position of authority and that of being a leader. I was beginning to learn.

Love,

Dad

From left to right, *Son Matt, Son David, sister Danna, David's wife Sarah, and my mother "DJ", Dorothy Jo Thompson*

Me speaking after first being sworn in as a Nebraska State Senator representing District #42

A Leap of Faith

My father, David F. Stevens Jr.

December 8, 2013

Dear David and Matt

If you recall from my previous letter I ended speaking of a time when everything became uncertain. At the same time there were clues my mind and my spirit's yearning to "be" were beginning to reconnect. It was as if my spirit had been hemmed in by my mind for so long but recent experiences were allowing it to assert itself more. And with that, new possibilities began to be nurtured and born.

A new reality was being formed but this time it was resonating from within and not just from my mind if that makes any sense. I was curious again. I *wanted* to know who I was and where I needed to go. And with each question and level of learning came new knowledge – knowledge that could only have been found by going *inward*. I had been looking in the wrong place for my answers. I had been looking "out there."

I will speak of these new ideas and ways of thinking later but suffice it to say I was learning not only how to think differently but how to create new realities. In fact I began to understand I could create any reality I wanted AND I could determine how I felt during any one moment in time.

I began to find myself, my core values and my purpose in life. Yet in the confusion of this beginning, I admit to often hearing a voice in my head saying, "Why are you thinking these things? This is stupid." But now there was another voice, the one saying, "It might be stupid, but there is no harm in exploring it a bit further. Besides, when looking at your life to date, what do you have to lose?"

For the first time in my life I sensed where I wanted to go and I began to learn I could create the mindsets and realities to make it happen. It was the first time I truly felt empowered as I began to understand and perhaps more importantly believe I had the tools within me to create meaning, purpose and joy in my life each and every day.

So when conservative Christians ask me if I have been "born again," I say "YES!" Yet it is the realization and context of the above I am referring to… for I truly was becoming empowered and a transformation was taking place. In every sense of the term I was being born again. Do I hear an AMEN?!

More importantly I knew I wanted to help others be empowered so they too, by their own thoughts and actions, could be the person they were created to be. I think I took to heart an old African saying, "Until one shows others who they truly are at their core being, they do not yet exist in the world." I knew I was beginning to truly exist for the first time and it felt really good.

I was changing from the inside out and was beginning to learn how to respond and create my present and future rather than just react and repeat what my experiences, culture and education had taught me. This change in thinking and understanding was the first critical piece needed for the rest to become possible. I know both of you have heard me say or read a post I may have written that speaks of the need to learn how to think differently. It is this I am referring to.

In order for anyone to face the challenges and changes always occurring in a chaotic universe, a shift in how we think must occur first. Otherwise we will simply take new information and process it while matching it with what we have learned from our past. For our mind really does not know the difference between what it sees and what it remembers.

If we are not aware of this basic truth we will continue repeating our past while under the mind-made illusion we are actually in control and thinking freely. We are not. What most people in the world experience is being trapped within their experiences and learning having never been able to break free. But enough of that for now...

                ಲ♡ಞ

Matt, I know you will remember the time period I am about to speak of. It was your final year of high school and around the time you "totaled" two cars and added some new dents in my CRV... and yes I know none were your fault! David, you were off in your own world of higher education creating music at the University of Nebraska, Lincoln.

As I was beginning to change and become more who I knew I was meant to be, I was given some outstanding advice by an adult student who had just finished taking the leadership program I had developed around the new concepts I had learned. So taking her advice, I traveled to California to be part of the CTI Co-Active Leadership Program. My classmates were 16 people from all over the world. It was a unique group and we would experience life, death, and rebirth together in terms of who we were and who we were to become.

For a bit of trivia, each group or class was given a tribe name. Some names for previous groups were: Lions, Lynx, Sharks, Whales, Condors, Eagles – all strong and cool names. For some reason the card overturned naming our group said Squirrels. Yep, so your dad and his fellow classmates from around the world became mighty

Squirrels and all I could think of most times were the numerous road kills of squirrels back home in Nebraska.

Toward the end of that program I had the privilege of going to Seoul, South Korea to co-lead a self-leadership workshop with Hae Sook Lee, an amazing woman and fellow Squirrel. It was my first experience teaching in another country with individuals whose culture was mostly unfamiliar to me. I loved it. I made mistakes to be sure, but the essence of what was taught was well received with the participants actually being disappointed we were not going to do more sessions or trainings in the future. It was my first taste of taking something I had helped create and teaching it at an international level and I knew I wanted more. And from what I saw, the world wanted more of it too.

I mention the above CTI Leadership Program for it was there in its concluding ceremony I made a commitment to myself and declared I was going out into the world to make a difference AND I was going to "play big" and not just play it safe anymore. In my heart I had always known I had been playing it safe throughout my life doing what came easily and naturally. That was soon going to change. I was going to go out into the world, wherever that might be, to help people learn for themselves their inner power to create their future along with the tools of self-leadership that would build the foundation for a life of meaning, purpose and joy, no matter what circumstances they may find themselves engulfed by.

And when I said I declared what I was going to do, it was an incredibly powerful personal experience. I vividly remember my fellow Squirrels standing together in an open area in the middle of the California Mountains surrounded by huge redwood trees under a clear night sky with stars shining in spectacular brilliance.

I do not remember much of the actual ceremony yet I do recall the moment when it was my turn to step out of the comfort of the circle and walk into the blackness of the night looking up into a brilliant star-filled sky. I remember feeling at one with the universe feeling… no, *knowing* I was not insignificant and that I was part of all, both seen and unseen.

I also remember looking out into the universe and shouting what it was I was determined to do in a voice that others said was dominating and commanding. I wasn't just telling myself or my classmates. I was telling the universe and God that I was going to do what deep down I had always had within me to do. I was declaring my willingness to lead by choosing the next steps, take them, follow my inner voice, combine that inner knowing with my full mind and body and to finally "be" who I was created to be while helping others find that same power within themselves.

I know God and the universe felt and heard the truth of my spirit that night. My spirit was both singing and at peace for the first time in a very long time.

And let me answer the question that I know popped into both of your minds as I was stating the above, "No, we were not smoking or drinking anything prior to that ceremony!" That being said, perhaps my originally saying that I "declared" was a slight *understatement* of what really happened that night. That night I began to "own" who I was and what I was going to do. I have never wavered far from my declaration that night under the California stars. I was beginning to understand the essence of what self-leadership truly is.

I do not wish to suggest to you everything in my life was now wonderful and my challenges gone. Such was definitely not the case as my life continued to unravel on the outside at the same time I was finding more stability within myself. My "significant other" I had been living with for nearly eight years decided that our staying together was not healthy for either of us. She was right I later recognized. We really did love each other I believe, but our pasts were such that we both seemed to trigger all too often the worst in each other by either something we said or some perceived action that was not received well or completely misunderstood. I learned sometimes love is not enough and that sometimes an environment can become so toxic that neither will survive and have the life they dreamed of having by remaining together.

So on one of my return trips from the California leadership trainings I came home to a lonely house and our separation was complete. I am happy to say we are still good friends and still communicate... probably better than we did before. Still, it was an unsettled time as you will recall, Matt.

By the way, David, you may not know this but Matt was really a lifesaver. He was staying at the time with your mom and your stepdad but when he knew I would be coming home but this time alone, he decided to move in to help ease the pain a bit. Between us I think Matt wanted to come to stay with me for various reasons but had not done so as he did not wish to hurt your mother's feelings. So my being alone was the excuse he needed to make that break. I will be forever grateful he did.

However, my life was continuing to unravel at an ever increasing rate. For the second time in my life I was fired. To be totally truthful, after 11 years as President of the Chamber, the board of directors had changed and the new majority had decided to go in a direction they believed I could not or would not go. Yet to this day I do not know the exact reasons for my being released as the Chamber's board decided not to tell me as it was deemed "confidential." I certainly have my suspicions but to say I truly know would be a lie.

Technically I wasn't fired. I was asked to resign and if I agreed I would receive a severance package in gratitude for my years of service to the Chamber, or I could refuse and be fired with no severance package. It was one of my easier decisions under the circumstances. I chose to resign.

Neither of you knows about the first time I was fired. I was paying my own way through college and working at a local burger fast food restaurant. I was leaving one evening and stated to one of my co-workers I was going to stop by a liquor store to get some wine and go to a party. She asked if I would do her a favor and pick her up a few bottles of wine as she too was going to a party after closing but the liquor stores would be closed by the time she was ready to go.

Being a nice guy and all I said yes, took her money and returned to the business with her wine. Little did I know she would decide to have the party there at the store with all of the other underage employees and the place would be left in shambles! Little did I know she was not of legal age at the time and that her father was the owner! Needless to say I was fired the next day.

At the time I "resigned" from the Chamber of Commerce, you David had married Sarah and you, Matt, were stuck living with a dad who was the talk of the town. One of the downsides of being a former Senator and Chamber President was that my personal life was clearly everyone's business.

Apparently, few believed I would just resign so suddenly. As such the rumor machines cranked up big time and rumors flew daily at a dizzying rate. People were talking and saying crazy things, especially in the "leave a comment" internet section of local media outlets which became particularly ripe with speculations. I think if both John Adams and Thomas Jefferson had been present during this time they would have felt perfectly at home as it compared nicely to much of what was fabricated about them during their service to people. I guess I can't complain as I am in good company. And after all it is what freedom of speech is all about and a right I worked hard to protect as a Senator even when what was being spoken was untrue and spiteful.

Some of the more interesting speculations were drug abuse, a criminal act on my part the Chamber wished to keep secret, or I had been forced out due to a power struggle because I would not go along with a group of community powerbrokers who wanted to control everything. I can't imagine what your life was like, Matt, with all this going on around you. It certainly did not add to any sense of stability we were striving to create, did it?

Tough and uncertain times they were and they just seemed to keep coming with no end in sight. And yet throughout it all was a growing sense within my spirit that I was on the right track if I could continue making choices that were in alignment with my values and continue to take steps in the direction I knew I needed to go. I sensed if I could do that and if I could keep my head somehow above the stormy waters I would find a way to survive.

Yet there was also another feeling lurking just beneath the surface of my emotions and thoughts. Something that kept alive a sense of foreboding where things might not turn out very well and that I was in deep trouble professionally, personally and financially while once again just pretending all was going to be fine. No matter how hard I tried to remain positive, I always sensed that thought to be close by and wanting to become stronger.

I decided to form my own small business of one and created Leader Development Group (LDG). As I was finding my way in a new business teaching authentic leadership I will admit to having great uncertainty and doubt whether I would make it. I almost didn't.

I was in my mid 50s by now and finding a job within the current environment of my being asked to resign and the disheartening rumors which seemed to pop up and become uglier each week became near impossible if I continued to live there. Part of me wanted to run and get away from it all. But you, Matt, were about to finish your senior year in high school so I decided if the new business was to grow it could be done from our small house by the lake where I felt somewhat isolated from the noise and more comfortable. Plus, I thought my leaving North Platte would be too disruptive for you whether you came with me or stayed there with your mom and stepdad.

In hindsight, Matt, I did not give you enough credit for being able to both adapt and to choose whether you wished to stay or to leave with me, probably going to Lincoln. I also think I used you as my reason for *not* doing anything and thus you became my justification for not taking a bold step. Still, it was not farfetched I might be able to grow the leadership teaching side of LDG. It also seemed possible I could develop international projects thus generating income with the help from contacts I had made throughout my life and the amazing things good use of social media could create.

I think it is also a fair statement that though I was beginning to change from within, there was much I needed to learn, particularly in how to think differently. So with all that was happening I was still stuck with only my experiences and past learning to help me make decisions, and those were all from the past. What I needed was a way to get out of my current mindsets and to grow the courage to leap from where I was into a new future.

But I was not there yet. I was stuck and I knew it and I seemed powerless to climb out of the hole I had fallen into. So I just hunkered down and tried harder which only created more of the same.

That is the thing about change. Most times it comes from out of the blue and is not compatible with the current ways of thinking. For me to beat this storm of change swirling around me, I needed to learn how to think differently and fast. Yet knowing that and doing it are two very different things for how does one learn to think in terms outside of what they know?

And though the persona I was exuding was one of "everything was going to be OK," I was not certain of that at all as the unraveling of my life continued with me just trying to hold on.

The economic meltdown and subsequent crash of the stock market took out most of my retirement. The housing market's crash a year or so later took the rest. So for me, there was very little in reserve and of course little income coming in as I was basically unemployed and the LDG business was just getting started. I was more than a little scared about what might happen.

By that time I had joined three of my fellow Squirrels in forming a new Canadian company called Hand-to-Hand Global Leadership (H2HGL) while still attempting to grow LDG. We had initially decided to create a program for youth in Jamaica as one of the members wanted to do something for his home country. This seemed a logical step for me as it was the international component I was looking for ever since the conclusion of the leadership program in California. I wanted to play big and forming a global company seemed to be a way to do that.

That partnership did not last long. Truth be told we could not get on the same page as to who to include in the core team and the issue of trust came front and center. In time, after originally working on a project for youth in Jamaica, the two others thought it best that I leave and I agreed.

That was a low moment as I was beginning to get a complex. My steps to move forward seemed to be going nowhere and too many relationships with people were failing. I began to wonder if I really was a failure but had simply been able to cover it up when things were on autopilot and easy.

What I was beginning to learn but did not realize yet was when a person begins to change and go a different path, the foundations of the old need to crumble away while a new one is carefully put in place. All around me my world was changing and in many ways I was just trying to hold on and keep my head above water. It was draining and nearly overwhelming at times as the fight to hang on was constant as the Northern Star. It never left and as such there was no peace. There was only uncertainty, worry, and turmoil both within and without as I fought to find some sense of stability.

My mind was frantically working, trying to find a way out of the hole I was in and at the same time my inner spirit was trying to shout that there is another way but I could not hear it very well. I could sense it but was unable or unwilling to pause long enough to listen as I was firmly "in my head" during that time. Yet I now see where I was making up so much within my mind based upon very little information, justifying actions like crazy while being extremely judgmental to everything and everyone.

In the end I do not believe I was seeing anything in its real sense during that period of change. Of course I *believed* I was seeing things clearly but I know now much of what I thought was true was simply made up from too little information and lack of perspectives.

There were times in there I seriously considered ending the fight to keep going especially during the low cycles. I considered it and a couple of times came close as I sped up the car I was driving on the highway heading to our home on the lake and nearly turned violently off the road and deliberately lost control. I came close… too close but obviously I did not complete those thoughts.

As the battle within my mind and spirit continued, my mind tried anything it could think of to help me survive my growing sense of panic while my spirit was saying the opposite: "Slow down! Calm down and listen! You are fine. We are fine. There is another way… another road we can follow!"

So perhaps out of desperation, I attempted to slow down and listen. As I did there was a growing sense within me I was getting stronger and things would be OK. As those thoughts continued to be fed, they grew and in time became part of my everyday experience. But at this time everything or something still seemed to be blocking each step I tried to take. I could not shake the thought that in everyone's dictionary the definition of "loser" just said: "See David F. Bernard-Stevens."

I was still doing small leadership trainings through the Leader Development Group but it was purely local in nature. Quite honestly I think there were many people thinking, based upon all of the rumors still swirling around, "He's teaching leadership? Maybe he should take a class on it himself!" And I must say, people were not exactly breaking down the door to take my program. I shall always have a place in my heart for those first brave souls who came to the leadership classes with open minds in the biggest sense of the word.

As I look back I can see there was a pattern to the chaos I was living. I was going down a path I could not see: I got my Master's Degree in Leadership from Bellevue University (online) after literally being "shoved" into doing something rather than just complaining. The man doing the shoving was Dr. Mike Chipps who was then the President of Mid-Plains Community College. My departure from the Chamber led me to create LDG thus beginning my pursuit of teaching empowerment and ethical leadership. My decision to become a Squirrel led me to form Hand-to-Hand Global Leadership with three of my colleagues which led me to the Director of Youth Services for the country of Jamaica and from there my first connection to Kenya. In the moment I saw nothing but chaos but there was a pattern in all of it I now see.

I do not know if it was all preordained or whether the patterns we weave when our minds and spirits are working hard to unite and create a positive future always end up in a beautiful collage. My sense is it is the second one but that will take a different letter I think.

Anyway, what seemed to be unsuccessful attempts to create a future were actually the foundational building blocks driving me toward the future I dreamed of having. Of course, as my dad used to say to me, "When one is ass up in alligators it is difficult to remember the original goal was to drain the swamp!" I thought it was a stupid saying at the time but now, not so much…

I was learning. The universe is indeed chaotic with good things happening to bad people and bad things happening to good people. Yet surrounding all of that chaos is an order. There were some rules and I was beginning to grasp this broader and more creative universe we all live in.

Let me end this letter by saying that the new foundation was being laid within me and it was guiding me toward an amazing adventure from which I would eventually discover who I was created to be and where I belonged. It is a journey everyone can and should take.

I have also learned that the journey each of us should take is never a given. We must choose to discover it for ourselves then choose to follow it. In all cases, we get to choose to follow the path that will make our lives meaningful and full of purpose and joy, or choose a different one with all the disappointments and uncertainties to be found there.

You and I get to choose thus being in the end totally accountable for the experiences of our lives. And with that knowledge is the beginning of true empowerment.

Love,
Dad

Some of those courageous souls who undertook my first leadership classes.

Those Mighty Squirrels

December 24, 2013

Dear David and Matt

I was thinking about both of you today and thought it time to continue my conversations about who your father is and perhaps more importantly, who he isn't. That sounded a little like *Star Wars*, didn't it, when Luke who did not know his true father, heard Darth Vader say, "Luke I am your father!"

Have I told you yet how proud I am of both of you? I am and I always have been even when both of you tried my patience and caused me to age faster than I should! And I have no doubt at times you both felt the same things about me!

I believe it is time to tell you about Jamaica whose gentle breezes seemed to whisper within my mind, "You have something to do and somewhere to go mon!"

Prior to the break-up, the team of Hand-to-Hand Global Leadership traveled to Jamaica with the idea of creating a youth empowerment and leadership program there. That is how I met Roberta Brown-Ellis, then the Director of Jamaica's Youth Services. The instant we met it was like seeing a long-lost friend. It felt as if I had known her forever. She was bright, inventive and passionate about her family, ethical leadership development and young people.

She was much younger than me yet I learned a great deal from her which would prove pivotal in my future decision making. She added a great deal to my thinking about how to create sustainable programs and to my surprise she expanded my thinking about spirituality and the need to decrease the distance between the mind and spirit. She always teased me about being too much in my head and I should get out of it more often to see things more clearly. To me she is someone who is young yet having an "old soul."

The H2HGL Jamaica project was a bold and aggressive plan to create authentic leaders from within Jamaica's youth. Sadly, due to the eventual break-up of the team, the developed project was never funded. Yet my going to Jamaica set the stage for what I was about to do and would become a powerful part of my ability to move forward. Perhaps that was the value of my choosing to be part of H2HGL. Perhaps that was the only path that would have taken me to Jamaica and later Africa. As I look back, it is a great example of how our choices do dictate to a large degree where we will go.

From the moment I set foot in Jamaica my world changed quickly and the path I needed to follow became much clearer... not easier necessarily but at least I was not meandering in the wilderness anymore. I would still stumble. I would still be knocked down and at times lose my way. Yet each time Roberta and so many others were there to pick me up, dust me off, yell at me a bit if needed and then with a smile and a distant virtual wave send me off again to do battle with the universe and what I intended to create within it while I still could. I realized I was not alone and that fact continued to give me courage and strength to go down this new path as far as I could in order to be and do what I believed I was created to do.

The planning we had done for the Jamaica project led someone in Canada to talk to someone they knew in Kenya about the concepts of empowerment and the leadership program the H2HGL team had been developing. In time, Mary Okioma, a Kenyan and leader of a small NGO, Women for Justice in Africa, contacted us via email. By us I mean Hand-to-Hand Global Leadership.

At that time Mary had been working with women in Kibera, which is one of the world's largest slums right in the heart of Nairobi. Specifically she was helping them cope with issues of physical and mental abuse. Yet her follow-ups showed that far too many had done nothing to help themselves. They had remembered their training but simply chose to stay in the same abusive situations.

Mary was hoping the program of teaching personal empowerment I had created at LDG and was helping to develop for Jamaica would be their answer.

As it turned out there was actually a member of the H2HGL team who had previously been in Nairobi working with women. She was selected as the lead contact between H2HGL and Mary. For various reasons, they were simply not able to connect consistently and since I was and still am most of the time on the internet, Mary was able to find me and we began to know more about each other and chat easily via Skype.

As I explained more of my own experiences, my teachings on mindsets and how they lock our actions in the present to the past, she became certain the program was needed in Kenya. We both believed if the women chose to change their own mindsets they would be ready to create something new – specifically a new present and thus a different future through their personal choices. With that new mindset, we believed future trainings in abuse would have more sustainability and resiliency. The initial key in the beginning wasn't the abuse training but their learning how to change their thinking and the creation of new mindsets.

It was shortly after returning from Tel Aviv when my leaving H2HGL occurred. I immediately contacted Mary and told her I was no longer associated with the company. I encouraged her to continue working with them as they were good people and could create an excellent program which would fit her needs. She flatly refused and though I'm sure the other team members assumed I stole their client, that was not the case. Mary stated I was the only one she had been able to talk to consistently and she liked where those discussions were leading and if I didn't mind she would continue talking to me thank you very much! And that, as they say, was that.

So we continued to talk and the magic of the universe began to show itself to me at last. It had always been there but I wasn't looking and my own mindsets clouded any chance of seeing things differently from what my experiences and learning had taught me.

And though I will speak of it later, many people believe our experiences are our best teacher. To some degree that is true, yet to a larger degree our experiences and what we have learned through others are also our own personal prison from which we constantly react and repeat our past within the context of current circumstances. Only when we recognize that and learn how to change from reacting and repeating into responding and creating can we make our own prison break and open our lives to infinite possibilities.

I was quickly learning how to do just that in my own personal life and I was about to make my own prison break very soon. I had no idea my break would lead me to Africa to meet a group of Kenyan women who not only brewed illegal alcohol but who would totally change my life... forever!

☙❧

I can't stress enough to the two of you how perilous my finances were during this time. As I think I mentioned earlier, the stock market crash had obliterated my portfolio with the eventual housing market bubble burst taking the rest. I suppose I could have been like many and simply walked into the bank, given them the keys and congratulated them on their owning a new house, but I just couldn't do that. It didn't fit into my core values damn it! So I continued to dip into what little savings I had until finally the house sold at a price close to the loan balance with all of the previously accrued equity long gone.

The good news was there were no more house payments. The bad news was I couldn't have made any type of payment anyway. The reality of being unemployed, middle-aged and attempting a totally new start-up that had a global scope with no start-up capital was very apparent and daunting within my mind. I remembered reading about people who had lost their jobs and struggled mightily only to end up losing everything including all self-respect. Now if I wasn't careful I realized I could easily become one of them.

It was a huge effort to recognize and ignore all I had been taught about what a successful man of my age looked like... for I was none of those things anymore. Instead, I was building and feeding new mindsets trying to create something new from seemingly nothing. In time, those mindsets would allow me to create so much more.

I learned all dreams and journeys start with a single step. I had heard this before and I too had stated so in speeches in my Senator and Chamber days. Now, however, I had a better understanding of its real meaning. I finally understood how impossible dreams and futures seem to be for most people in the world. Where before I had it all and it all came so easily, now I had nothing and everything I tried seemed destined to run into a brick wall or two. I had created a life where one chooses to let go of their dreams as the need of just knowing how to survive becomes the front and center of everything.

I now understood how overwhelming trying to change the course of one's life really is for millions around the planet. For them, taking the next step is simply another step to nowhere which will amount to nothing different. Yet they take another step in order to survive... until they choose not to take another step and all that choice brings with it. I totally believe too many in the world die not because it was "their time" but because they simply became tired of the fight. And let's face it, life is a fight whether it is to create our dreams or to simply survive. Life knows no bounds and is not judgmental. It doesn't pick and choose who to aid or who to hurt... it just keeps pounding on us creating circumstance after circumstance 24/7. It never stops.

Finding the strength to endure that kind of punishment and incessant pounding can only be found by going within ourselves to find that flame placed within us at the moment of our creation. It is the flame within that when fed can provide us with the power and the energy to not only endure, but to create and make our lives worthwhile. Without the power found within that flame, life can and will become overwhelming and meaningless.

It was about this time when I discovered an amazing thing. Our thoughts really do matter as they create and attract things of equal value. This is true for both positive and negative thoughts. I was learning that by linking my thoughts to my core values and purpose, there was a power within me I never knew nor comprehended and when unleashed, not only would the universe respond but amazing things would happen.

Perhaps most importantly, I learned just thinking of all that needed to be done to create a dream or just to move forward can become overwhelming and eventually leads to a paralysis of thought and action. To prevent that paralysis, I found I had to focus solely on the next step while keeping it in line with my values and the path I needed to follow.

In doing so I discovered a simple truth. Taking the next step was all I or anyone could do at any one time anyway so why not just strive to do that and not worry about all the other steps one will need to take later? I could do that – just take the next step with each step being manageable and certainly not overwhelming as when thinking of the entire journey.

I also discovered I would at times be knocked down and pushed back a few steps for it is a very chaotic world out there. Yet whenever that happens all I need do is get up, shake my head and say something like, "Wow! I didn't see that coming!" and take my next step *from wherever I landed.* And the wonderful part is that with each step taken a sense of meaning, purpose and joy comes as we become aware of our walking the path we were meant to walk.

This is important for no matter what life throws our way, we can always take the next step from where we landed and with each step is an inner joy… thus the steps upon which any journey is created is where our meaning and joy come from, not the end or outcome. And with this knowledge I once again began inching toward a dream instead of just surviving another day. And I was doing it one step at a time.

This is what so many people in the world who have had such a powerful impact have done. They too had a vision or a dream yet all that needed to be done to achieve it seemed overwhelming to them too. All they could do was to take their next step. And when they were knocked down, jailed, suffered through broken relationships, fired, financially ruined or otherwise stopped, they simply took the next step from where they landed in the direction they had always intended to go with each choice being aligned with what they valued most.

Knowing the above was easy for me. Understanding it at a deeper level was a different story. Yet all this is the same for each of us, including you. So who do you wish to be? Where do you wish to go that will give the most joy, passion and meaning? What is your next step you need to take to make that happen? Then the hardest of all to do, choosing to actually take that step and letting go of the past.

For me that next step was going to be a doozy and it would in the end define forever within my spirit and mind what a leap of faith truly is in life. As a fellow Squirrel once said to me, "The journey itself will be a wild ride and the only one worth taking, but watch that first step because it's a doozy!" She was right...

For me that first step came when Mary requested me to come to Kenya to train 80 women from Kibera, Africa's largest slum, in a program for empowerment and self-leadership. However there was a big problem. Mary's NGO, Women for Justice in Africa (WOJA), was very small and had no funds at that moment to pay for the training. And as I was to find out, the poor in Kenya don't pay to come to training, which was totally contrary to my life in the United States where people paid me for the chance to learn what I had to teach.

In Kenya and in most of the developing world, those doing the training have to pay the participants a "transport fee" so that they can afford to come and go home. Those doing the training also need to provide morning and afternoon teas, a good lunch, and a per diem for participants as some may have to close their small business in order to attend. The per diem would help make up any potential loss while they were attending the training. This is the system that has been created over time in Kenya and has become the norm participants expect before deciding to attend.

I will speak of the dysfunctional process this has created over time a bit later but for now the cost of my going and doing the training for these women was a lot, and like Mary, I had nothing financially to bring to the table. Even if I had, there would be no way to be refunded as all funds would flow to the participants with nothing coming back. In most cases an NGO would get a grant or the "donors" would pay for the expenses – but there was no grant, there were no donors.

As Mary and I talked, we thought about various ways to raise the money, some not far removed from having a bake sale. Mary thought since the new American

President had roots in Kenya, many Americans would want to come and see where their new President's roots were; thus we could set up the many tours and use the income from those to fund the training.

I laughed inwardly at that and had to explain to someone who was very proud of a man born from Kenyan roots who had risen to become President of the United States that, for the most part, Americans were still arguing whether President Obama actually had a legitimate American birth certificate and whether or not he was a Muslim terrorist at heart! Needless to say there were no tours pending or any other answers that would bring the money needed.

And then it happened.

Your Grandmother DJ had offered me a room to stay in her home in Lincoln until things settled down (yes your father had to go stay with his mom when there were no other alternatives available... depressingly true!). This was of course after the two of you were gone and the house had sold.

As such I was driving from North Platte to Lincoln when, after talking with a friend about whether I should try to go to Kenya, it hit me. It was as if a tidal wave of certainty had washed over my entire body. It came from out of nowhere and was nothing like I had ever experienced before or since. At that moment I *knew* I was supposed to go to Kenya.

I also *knew* two other things: one, upon going my life would never be the same, and two, I would experience poverty more than at any time of my life – not just by seeing it but by *being* it. It was as if an ancient oracle was speaking to me and telling me my future, which in this case ended up being true in every detail.

So I had a decision to make. On the one hand my spirit was saying I must go to Kenya, that the road to my purpose and dream would begin there. On the other hand all I had experienced, learned and otherwise stored within my mind was saying it was stupid to go to Kenya. It would cost me all the remaining money I had and if I used credit cards would actually put me further into debt with no real income yet at this point. There was no guarantee of any return on investment, Africa was a total unknown and, according to everyone including the U.S. State Department, Nairobi was a dangerous city for an American to be in. In fact, our government had listed Nairobi as *the* most dangerous city in the world at the time for traveling Americans.

Yet at a deep level I knew I was supposed to go to Kenya.

So, as you will have at various times in your lives, I had a choice to make. I could play it safe or take a leap of faith. Obviously I decided to leap and it was then I first began to understand the meaning of the phrase "taking a leap of faith is to have faith."

It was a leap of faith because there were literally no guarantees of any success whatsoever. Yet there was a deeper sense within my spirit that I would be OK. *Now I want to be clear on this... it was not that I would not fail or that all would turn out like I dreamed it would. The knowing my spirit was giving me was that the essence of who I was at my core would be OK. I would survive and I would take the next step no matter where or how I landed.*

So I called Mary and told her I was coming. She was so excited and it was for her as if God had moved mountains... and perhaps he or she had! We worked out when I should arrive and some of the logistical details WOJA needed to do prior to my arrival. I also said I would like to work with some young people while I was there. Then she asked the inevitable question, "How did you get the money?"

When I told her I didn't have it but was coming anyway and getting my ticket as soon as our conversation ended, there was a really long silence on her end of the line. In the end I suspect she decided she could cancel everything at the last moment and limit WOJA's exposure to any financial risk so she said OK as long as I was certain.

And that was that.

I got my ticket via credit card that day and I was committed to go to Kenya with no way of paying for what was to come. Parts of me – OK, a big part of me – said, "David, what the hell are you doing?" But another part, not in my mind but coming from deep within said, "You are supposed to go to Kenya. You will be OK no matter what happens. Have faith." I felt a growing sense of excitement and a lurking fear at the same time.

"And though I walk through the valley of the shadow of death I shall fear no evil for thou art with me..." kept coming into my consciousness. (Psalm 23:4)

I was beginning to understand what many of the great philosophers had said throughout the millennia – that God was within us not outside of us. It was as if I heard what Luke had to say in his Chapter 17 verses 20-21 when he spoke of Christ talking about the kingdom of Heaven. In essence he quoted Jesus as saying that people will look for heaven over there or up there but it is in none of those places. "... for the kingdom of Heaven is within you."

For the first time I was beginning to sense and acknowledge the power I had within and I was beginning to learn how to listen and tap into its energy. Some may call that power Allah, or Yahweh, God, the Great Spirit or Universal Consciousness but whatever the name for it, it truly is there just as the ancients knew.

I was shocked as to what happened next and I began to learn by new experiences what can be attracted via one's thoughts and actions. And the new mindsets forming my new reality began to grow exponentially, or so it seemed.

I was talking to a good friend, Jane Chin, via social media and told her the choice I had just made to go to Kenya and the reasons behind that choice. She immediately took the time to set up an income-generating account on my website and told me to tell my story on both my blog at the time and via social media. I did so, telling anyone who wished to read what I was doing, where I was going, why and the fact I had no clue how I was going to do it. I stated I was determined to go on this adventure if anyone was willing to help a middle-aged man finally going after his dream, that would be amazing… or something like that.

Within three weeks the money had come from people living all over the world to fund the trainings. Some from longtime friends, some from people I did not know and of course some from those mighty Squirrels.

I cannot emphasize how amazing that was! Clearly, when one takes a leap of faith and it is aligned to core values and purpose, the universe will respond in ways one cannot imagine. Some will experience these things and call it magic. Others will call them miracles. For me these experiences are simply how God created the universe, as we are beginning to understand both spiritually and scientifically.

To put it another way, the new Spock of *Star Trek* may have been right when he stated, "There are no such things as miracles" Yet from my experience what the universe can create with us via our thoughts and actions may surely feel like one would expect from being within a miracle!

By creating new mindsets I changed my reality from being "don't do anything rash and play it safe" into making choices to go into an unknown where I knew I was supposed to be. And with that I began unleashing an unlimited number of possibilities into my life and reality.

I was learning how to let go from attempting to control my outcomes to match what most would deem to be acceptable, to allowing the universe to work with my thoughts and choices and respond to the outcomes created. I was also beginning to understand there were times I needed to simply let go and ride the current to where it was going to take me. Still making decisions mind you, just not trying to control *everything*, which is not possible anyway.

However, I will tell the two of you that letting go conflicted with a long-held mindset that a leader controlled his or her outcomes. I was taught good leaders got what they wanted by always finding a way through true grit, commitment, persistence, determination and force of will. Almost too late in my life I discovered these bits of information to be extremely misleading.

Those things are part of what an individual may "put out into the universe" but the outcomes will be created by so many other things making our part of determining those outcomes just that: only a part. However, letting go of the power this mindset had on me has been a tough one and it still challenges me today. Yet I can also tell you that *every time* I get back into that controlling mindset, things do not go as well and the more I let go, the better things become.

I am still working on letting go but I am getting better.

For the first time in a very, very long time I felt I was doing things right and going down the path I had always needed to travel. I was in my mid 50s by that time so obviously your dad must have been a slow learner! But of course that is not true. I think for me, the road I chose was the road I needed to take leading me to a time where my choices of action or inaction would put me in a position where I would have to choose to leap or stay the course. The choice was mine alone to make.

Who knows whether I was at a similar point in my life at an earlier age? If I was, I wasn't ready for it or was totally unaware of the importance of that moment or choice. Did I choose wrong or right years ago? The answer to those questions is that it doesn't matter. We are where we have landed at any one point in time and it is from there we will take that next choice and step either toward our dream or further away.

I think most people have those moments. Sadly, most choose to stay the course and for them each day will be like the day before until there simply are no more days left. For others they will not see their moment of choice and totally miss the chance to be and go to where their dreams could have been made.

For them, the road of their dream will be the road never taken and in time the dream they once had will be forgotten, unfed and nearly dead. I say "nearly" as all dreams are never totally dead as anyone can jumpstart their dream whenever they choose no matter how old they may be. It is simply a matter of choice and the taking of that first step.

What are your dreams, my intelligent sons? Do you know or have you forgotten? Either way, just remember your father showed you it is never too late to choose to follow the path of one's dreams. For it is true, it is not the obtaining of the dream that matters in the end but the journey itself. It is the journey and the manner one walks it where all joy and meaning emanates. Perhaps that is where capitalism's quest for material wealth has done much harm to the human spirit... but that might be for another letter.

When I write next I will tell you what happened when I arrived and how indeed everything changed including my becoming even poorer than I was prior to coming here to Kenya! I know, who would have thought that was even possible!

*love you both
so much,*
                        Dad

The Hand-to-Hand Global Leadership Team **(with Roberta Brown-Ellis on my immediate left).**

A Leap of Faith

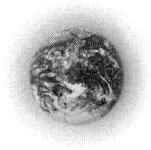

January 22, 2014

Dear David and Matt

It has been a perfect day here in Nairobi. Ruth, who I haven't spoken of yet but who you both know is my wife now, is upcountry being the construction manager on a women's group zero-grazing dairy facility. Anyway, as I was cooking myself some dinner I was reminded that Ruth is a member of the Kalenjin tribe and it is their culture that men should NOT be in the jikoni (kitchen) at any time unless their wife is sick or otherwise absent. Then and only then is it OK for a married man to cook. The same is true for helping with household chores.

You would think that I would be in seventh heaven as there is no pressure ever put upon me when we are together about helping to cook, clean the house or wash dishes. I can just sit in the sitting room reading or taking a nap until Ruth or the girls fix me my dinner. But your Grandmother DJ taught me too well and I just have a hard time doing it. Helping out in the home and kitchen is a very strong mindset within me!

In fact, in the beginning when in our rural home in Kenya, I would actually get in the jikoni and try to help. Ruth would protest but I kept thinking in time she would see my value and it would be a time where we could talk and do things together. That was my American (Nebraskan) mindset at play and I *knew* in time she and everyone else would see it my way as it was of course… the right way! I envisioned after a bit of time all men and women in the area happily working and talking together in their jikoni forever more!

I was wrong. It was Mary (Okioma) who finally set me straight. I was telling her of my attempts to help Ruth cook and she finally just stopped and asked, "Why do you wish to embarrass her in front of her friends and elders?" I think I said something to the tune I was not embarrassing anyone but showing by example what men and women can do to help each other and build upon their relationships. Finally Mary just said, "Look that is nice of you and very Nebraskan but this is not Nebraska. The only thing people are thinking when they see you helping Ruth is how terrible a wife she must be. She is obviously so bad at cooking and keeping house even her husband has to help her!"

Thus began the continuation of my learning about mindsets and what people react to and think is right or wrong from what they have learned in their past. In fact, the actual impact of my trying to change the perception of what men could do in the kitchen and house was that my way, that is to say the American way, was right and theirs was wrong and inferior. So I adjusted and so has Ruth. Now, when we are in Nairobi, she will let me help *a little bit* and she knows when she is in America I might even cook the entire meal! But when we are in our Center Kwanza near Jua Kali, it is her kitchen to cook in and house to clean! Life truly is fascinating…

But let me get back to my story to you. I think I was just about ready to leave for Africa and Ruth and I were still many choices away from meeting.

I admit to not knowing for certain where Kenya was but I was pretty sure it was somewhere in East Africa. I knew that Swahili and English were the accepted national languages and most in the rural areas would only know their tribal mother tongue as many were not able to go to school due to their parent's inability or choice not to pay school fees. It has only been the past few years where primary school became free by law here in Kenya although parents still need to fund uniforms, books, some teacher fees, and lunch the school may provide. And even with the primary tuition now being free, far too many primary students are not attending.

The point being that with the women I would be training in Nairobi, I would be using an interpreter who would translate my English into Swahili and others would step in to help translate into various mother tongues for those not understanding either English or Swahili. That's about the extent of what I knew about Kenya – oh and they had lions and elephants, it was along the equator and apparently had some very nice weather at times.

OK, I'll also admit to some stupidity as well, as in my mind I *knew* the planet's equator went through the heart of Kenya. And so I also expected to experience monsoon rains, high heat and humidity, hordes of bugs and dense jungles. I was worried as to how I would hold up under the intense heat. As I later found out, the only place where I would find what I expected around the equator in Kenya was within my own mind. Only one word suffices to explain that one… DUH!

When I landed in Nairobi it was late in the evening. Mary picked me up at the airport with Leonard Kiniti aka Chege driving his taxi. It had just rained and I commented upon taking my first breath of real African air, "Wow! Everything smells so clean and fresh!" They both kind of just stared at the silly American Mzungu (white faced person) and I remember Mary stating something to the tune of, "This is Nairobi, David, the smoke from all of the truck exhausts will probably kill you over time."

Ahh yes, welcome to Africa and it was clear from the get-go I had not a clue what I was doing. As I would quickly discover, much of what I had learned from my life in the United States would not help either.

I stayed the first two weeks with Mary, her mother and family. Mary's mother Helen was the true matron of the home as her husband had married a second wife many years prior and stayed with the second wife and the children from that marriage. Polygamy was something I should have realized existed in Kenya but somehow that little gem escaped me as I was preparing to come. I soon discovered that *nothing* of what I expected to find would actually exist in the manner I expected.

Their apartment consisted of a small but adequate kitchen, a large sitting/dining room, two full baths, and four bedrooms. All in all there were up to five children in the Okioma family in Kenya, three children abroad, a plethora of friends, Helen and her father who was ill and needing care and a house girl who would all be staying in the house at any one time. I was given a room all to myself only learning later that it had been Mary's. She had graciously given it up for me and she slept on a mattress on the floor of her mother's larger master bedroom as that was the only spare place available.

They were and are an amazing close-knit family and it was a blessing I was able to spend time with them. In fact, I ended up staying with them for most of the first two years of my stay, paying rent in time so as to keep me from being a burden.

They are an amazing family and they allowed my introduction to Kenya to be gradual and well grounded. They truly were my Kenyan family away from home and I will always have a special love in my heart for each of them including those extended family members in the United States and Canada.

~ ~

So I arrived and quickly an amazing thing happened. I had been introduced to two outstanding young people via Rhea D'Souza, a woman from India who knew via the internet I wanted to work with young people while I was in Kenya. And so it was that Steve Kimaru and Ann Njeri (now Ann Njeri Kimathi) became part of my life. As Mary departed quickly to attend a conference in the United States, Steve and Ann picked me up and thus started my beginning introduction to the real Kenya and the challenges faced by youth throughout the country.

I stayed with each of them as they set up through their networks leadership trainings where I would reach over 400 young Kenyans over the next few weeks. But unbeknownst to me, I soon discovered they were part of the Initiatives of Change advance team for Professor Rajmohan Gandhi's upcoming trip to Kenya, who of course is the grandson of Mahatma Gandhi.

You can imagine the smile on my face when they asked if I cared to tag along as their planning team was to meet at an accountant's office in Nairobi. I ended up meeting some of the most professional and dedicated people I have ever met in terms of working hard to bring real change into the world. I had never heard of Initiatives of Change let alone what they were attempting to do in the world but the more I learned, the more it resonated within me.

On arrival, the Gandhi team consisted of mostly young people from around the world between the ages 25 to 35. In his own right Professor Gandhi is someone worth spending time with. He and his team adopted me right away and I remember being thrilled as a school boy when he introduced me by name to a large group as part of his team. There was a kindness to him and yet a deep knowledge as well as to the need of finding ways of bringing people together to create peace, reconciliation and ethical leadership.

Through Steve, Ann and the Initiatives of Change team I had the opportunity to speak with over 1,000 young people throughout the Rift Valley area and Nairobi. Wherever I spoke, my message was well received and everyone wanted more. The thought began forming within my mind that my stay in Kenya may not be just for five weeks.

As an aside, it was through meeting the Initiatives of Change team that four years later Ruth and I would be invited to travel to Panchgani, India joining Rhea D'Souza to speak and be part of two conferences on Ethical Leadership at the Initiatives of Change Conference and Training Center. The circle was completed as I was the moderator of a panel discussion which Professor Gandhi was part of. This time, I introduced him to the audience! I doubt he was as giddy as I was for his introduction of me but it was still pretty cool!

Back to Steve and Ann for a moment, I had many first experiences with them. First matatu rides where safe driving is only a suggestion. First shuttle into the unknown Kenyan countryside. First having a taxi breakdown in the middle of the night in the middle of nowhere and *definitely* the first time being asked to hide on the back seat while being covered up by clothes so word would not spread there was a Mzungu stuck on the road which might lead to thugs coming to rob everyone!

Another first was experienced during the first night I stayed in the home of Steve's parents. They had set me up in a very comfortable guest room and Steve quickly showed me where everything was. I soon discovered I should have paid a bit more attention.

I remember noting the shower area and there being a porcelain toilet sunken into the floor flush with the surface. Again, I didn't think too much about it until I had to use the bathroom a bit later. I learned a bit more about mindsets that night.

As I suspect you have heard me say a time or two, mindsets are the memories within our mind's database collected over time from our experiences and what we have learned in various ways. Attached to each memory is an emotion and together they help us explain or interpret the world around us – at least from the limited view of what we know. I say limited because when I compare what I know to what I don't know in the universe, what I know looks more like an atom on top of a pin head in comparison. OK, I admit that the pin head wasn't needed as the atom would still be the same size but somehow it seemed so much smaller with it added!

Anyway, I had to go "number 2" in our vernacular, "long call" here in Kenya, and finally began looking at the bathroom area with a higher sense of purpose.

So as my eyes stared at the photons being reflected from the sunken toilet, my mind was doing a deep Google search of my vast data storage base desperately attempting to match the information the eyes were sending its way. It was coming up with nothing... zero, zip, nada. The only match it could come up with was to do what I had been taught to do back in Nebraska. Armed with that memory I proceeded to sit on the floor over the toilet and did my thing. All ended up well and I was kind of proud of myself for figuring it all out, strange as the experience was.

It was perhaps a year or so later I finally told that story to Mary and her family one evening over dinner. Their reaction really surprised me. Perhaps the best way to describe it is to say three words: uncontrolled hysterical laughter. Tears were flowing from their eyes as they asked me again, "You actually sat on the floor of the toilet to go to the bathroom??!!" My confirming my actions once again set off new waves of laughter toward the smart but culturally naive Mzungu.

It was then it was explained to me how to squat and it was there I was told that most toilets in rural

Kenya were merely holes in the ground and where sitting on the floor would be incredibly unsanitary! Of course, everyone being an educated lot, the irony of the developing country's citizens explaining to the "developed" citizen about good sanitation was not overlooked! What fun they had at my expense and I, though initially embarrassed, had fun as well as it was all part of learning new things.

But the real reason for my coming to Kenya, the training of the women from Kibera, was finally fast approaching. I was about to find out if a man from rural Nebraska could create an environment where women who had been abused both physically and mentally in so many ways by other men would be willing to share openly with each other and to me, another man.

Some very smart people told me by my being a man, the women would not open up to me because they would not trust me completely. And even if they did, as a man I would be unable to understand their real challenges. I did not agree of course yet I also accepted the possibility they might be right. Regardless, I was about to find out.

Mary's small NGO had been doing trainings for women in the slum of Kibera in the area of abuse and how to deal with it. As I stated earlier, when they began their follow-ups, they discovered that far too many had not changed their circumstances and were still in the same abusive situations.

Not surprisingly, Mary and her team were asking themselves "why?" Was their teaching inadequate? Were the women not serious in wanting to end their abuse? What was it?

In time they discovered their training had been good as each woman knew what to do, who to call if needed and the support groups and organizations available to help. They had stayed in their abusive and spirit-crushing environment because they *chose to do so!*

But why? Why would a woman who knew there was help available for her stay within a terribly abusive environment? Was it because they did not feel empowered? Was it because they lacked the tools to lead themselves successfully? They were questions that deserved answers.

During the trainings with the women I found basically three reasons for their not leaving the abusive situation they were in:

- They did not believe anything they did would matter in the end. In fact many believed that trying to escape the abuse would only make things worse.
- Some believed the abuse they were suffering was their punishment for some unknown sin in the eyes of God. In their mind (mindset) they believed their God was merciful and as such they could not rectify that with their daily misery. So it was a choice that either God was merciful and

good or he was not. Since to them God was still merciful and good, the only reason God must be allowing their abuse is they had somehow sinned terribly in the eyes of God and the abuse they were experiencing was their punishment. *Thus theirs was to endure God's wrath* as getting out of their punishment would in their view only make things worse in the eyes of God.

- They were frightened about what might happen to them and their children if they left their abusive situation which in most cases was still the only source of financial support in their lives, paltry as it was.

And with those mindsets and subsequent thoughts, everything they experienced each day was seen through that lens and through that lens was created their world view. Their thoughts created their reality and their choices springing from that reality created exactly who they believed they were – unworthy.

Do either of you remember one of the prayers we used to say in some of the Episcopal (Anglican in Kenya) services you grew up in? At that time many used what is now called Rite One which is still used today in some parts of the world. It is referred to as the Prayer of Humble Access and was said by the congregation just prior to receiving the holy sacrament of communion. The sense of the women of their own worth reminded me of this prayer and how so many people are reinforced in so many ways of their being unworthy. And what we reinforce and feed will grow even if it is our fears or the mindsets of being unworthy. The traditional wording of the prayer went like this:

> We do not presume to come to this thy Table O merciful Lord trusting in our own righteousness, but in thy manifold and great mercies. *We are not worthy so much as to gather up the crumbs under thy Table.* But thou art the same Lord, whose property is always to have mercy: Grant us therefore, gracious Lord, so to eat the Flesh of thy dear Son Jesus Christ, and to drink his Blood, in these holy Mysteries, that we may continually dwell in him, and he in us, that our sinful bodies may be made clean by his Body, and our souls washed through his most precious Blood. Amen.

Cannibalistic references aside, don't you find it interesting that any church would devise a prayer of that nature… one that would continually reinforce our unworthiness? Perhaps I am an idiot but I for one do not believe for one moment that the message of Christ in his teachings which in time became Christianity would have been preaching anything but *empowerment*. Everyone was worthy, even those called in those days "untouchables!" But that is an issue for another letter perhaps.

January 22, 2014

I will not go into great detail the program I did for the women of Kibera. Suffice it to say that before any empowerment could be done or thoughts of self-leadership could develop, there had to be a change in thinking. And over a five-day period that is exactly what happened.

After learning about mindsets and how it is possible to create any reality desired, each woman was asked to think about who they believed they were as a person. When they returned the next day you could hear a pin drop as each began to tell their story and why they were convinced that they were not a good person and not worthy. For many they were tearfully sharing their story for the first time. That was a good beginning for as individuals share with others they begin to own their lives rather than the experiences and perceptions of their lives owning them.

At the end of that day I asked each woman to find some time that evening to look again upon their reflection in a mirror and again ask who they were. This time I said I wanted them to look harder and to go deeper to find the real answer and not just those things which came to them from the mindsets of their mind when they first asked the question of themselves. When they returned the next day it was one of the most magical experiences of my life.

We were all sitting around in a large oval facing each other in the small rectangular training room. There were no tables and the lights were off with only the natural light from the sliding glass doors in the room. I simply asked who was willing to share what they had found. There was a *long* silence which seemed to last an hour though in fact it was probably only about three to five minutes. And then it happened.

One woman stood up and said she would like to say something. She stated at first she did not understand why Daudi (David in Swahili) would be asking her to do something she had already done. And why would he want her to think again about things that were so painful to think about? Then she said she remembered I asked her to go deeper and though she wasn't sure exactly what that meant, she began to think again about who she was and begin to ask herself, "Is that really true? Is that really who I am?"

I will never forget what came next. With a voice growing in confidence and intensity, she restated what she had said yesterday about who she was. Then she very firmly said that was a lie and not her at all. She was not a failure or worthless. And then she began to list who she really was at her core. She stated she was kind, compassionate, hard-working, a good mother, and she was both honest and trustworthy – and she said it with such confidence and passion! She was amazing. All I could say when she was finished was, "Yes, you are."

From that moment on the sound of silence was never heard again as each in turn stated more of the same in terms of their own personal discoveries. What these brave explorers had found was their treasure – their truth and not the one that had been created within their heads by their experiences and what they had learned from others.

And the smiles were contagious with an energy filling the room like nothing I had ever experienced before. It was the energy of transformation. It was the energy of relief, joy and yes, of grieving too. It was the energy of new-found life and a growing sense of something different happening in their lives. I knew that sense for I was going through it myself.

I was fortunate to have Joan Fitzpatrick, a wonderful woman from Canada, helping me for two of the three groups. Joan flew to Kenya at her own expense and with no compensation to help me with the training. She had also helped raise funds for the training dollars needed I spoke of before with many of her friends in Canada reaching out to help. The first day we met in person was when she landed. Together we created "on the fly" – an exercise that would symbolically show the letting go of the past and entering the new world of the present and thus future.

There was a fence with a gate separating the outside of the training room with a parking lot. The women stood as a group on one side of the fence with each taking their turn stating for all to hear what their minds had told them they were, based upon their experiences and from what they had previously been taught.

Then, with each stating firmly and confidently who they knew they truly were from the core of their being, they individually walked through the gate, waved farewell to let go of their past mindsets and stepped into the new reality of their life. It was a very moving experience and as the number of women increased on the other side of the gate, the cheers for each new woman entering that new reality became louder and louder with much singing and dancing for each choosing to "cross over into their light."

Rebirth from death... it is a theme within stories running throughout mankind's history and it was coming into being for these women from the slum of Kibera just as it was coming into being for me.

What we think and the mindsets we create are powerful. They define who we are and to a large degree where we will go. We can have the world define who we are for us or we can go within ourselves to ask the deeper questions of ourselves. Trust me; the world does not know who you are... only you do. And when you go deep, work hard, ask the tough questions such as "do I really know that to be true?" while answering them with brutal honesty without judgment, the emerging answers can change everything.

As the women eventually discovered, finding who they truly were was an incredibly important first step.

However, their next step would be more difficult. The next step would be their choosing whether or not to "be" the person they knew themselves to be.

In this case, "being" meant starting that day to align both their thoughts and actions with who they knew themselves to be. They would show they were honest by being honest. They would show they were compassionate or kind by being compassionate or kind. To say it another way, their behavior would be guided by their "being" through their actions stemming from who they understood they were created to be.

It was their first taste of true self-leadership and from my own experience it tastes like nothing experienced before. Each was responding to create in their life that which they knew themselves to be and not just reacting and behaving to that which they "thought" they were. Their first test came quickly as their assignment was to "be" who they were created to be in both their thinking and actions upon going home.

The next day we talked about their experiences of attempting to "be" who they knew they were as a human being. Two stories stick out in my mind. One woman I will name Florence said how much she hated her neighbor. They avoided each other like the plague and had not spoken to each other for years. Florence decided that since she knew herself to be a loving person, hating her neighbor was not the right thing for her to do. So she planned her next step in order to "be" by her thoughts and actions the kind of person she knew herself to be.

As it turned out, the hated neighbor stepped outside early that evening. Florence went up to her, reached out to take her hand into her own and stated how sorry she was for her behavior toward her for so long. Apparently the person was stunned and did not know what to say. After a moment, the neighbor said she too was sorry and they both started talking about their lives and how difficult things had been. Florence said a friendship was built that night and everything changed. The stress and anger were gone as they were replaced by compassion, love and joy.

The second story took my breath away. A woman I'll call Halyma talked about how angry she was toward her sister who had died a year ago. She was angry because her sister's children were now all her responsibility at a time when she was barely keeping things together for her own children.

Halyma said, "I was angry at my sister for dying and I was angry at her children for being in my house making my life more difficult." She stated how terrible she was to her sister's children and how tense things always were when she and the children were together. But, "Yesterday," she said, "I knew I was compassionate at my core and it dawned on me how I had been anything but compassionate to the children of my sister."

That night, she decided to gather everyone in their small home in the Kibera slums to talk to the entire "family" all at once. Halyma stated she told them everything: how angry she had been at her sister for dying and how angry and frustrated she was when her children came to her house. She told us that she started to cry as she told each of them how sorry she was and that she was going to be a better mother as she understood that everything had not been easy for them either and they too might be angry about things. She also said that she loved each of them very much and gave each child a hug of their very own.

She paused a moment to gather herself as the tears had begun flowing while speaking of her experience. Finally she looked up and said the change was immediate. Everyone in her family had tears but they were tears of joy and everyone hugged each other in a warm embrace as families do when things are tough and they need each other to survive. She said the tension vanished and that everything changed... everything. She also said that forgiveness to her sister was immediate and permanent.

Thus ended the trainings and the reason I initially came to Kenya. I wish I could transfer to you what it felt like to be part of those trainings with the amazing women who had suffered so much and had so little. I think the best way for me to describe it is to ask you to think of a time your spirit was totally engaged in something. David, perhaps it is when you were writing some of your creative pieces for orchestra. Matt, perhaps it was when you were helping your Grandpa Jess on the farm growing food for the world. Those times in your life where you felt so much joy, contentment, passion and a sense of being alive is what my experience was with the women of Kibera.

I shed tears with them, I was frustrated along with them and I felt deep compassion and a strong connection through a single purpose: wishing to find joy, meaning and a way of being more than I was before. It is like a drug which makes one feel wonderful, and like a drug, once I felt what was created within the training I wanted more of it. It is addictive but in a good way I think for the more I get that feeling, the more I have touched others and pushed them to becoming better leaders of themselves and with others.

I want to add here that as the women were taking their self-leadership journey, I too was continuing my own leadership journey through them. As I wondered if the women would openly share their truth, I wondered if I would open myself up to others and share my own truths. And I want to say this, the pain and exhilaration the women found in their sharing, I too would find in my own time.

It is still hard for me to talk openly about my past to others as there are still the lingering remnants of previous mindsets and the reactions which still tempt me at times today. For though I have not been feeding them and they have been reduced in their power, they are still there and need to be dealt with from time to time.

As an example, as I thought about whether to state some of the personal experiences of my own life to the women during the trainings, there were still strong reactions and thoughts saying, "It is nobody's business! It is personal and sharing will only make people think the worst." Or, the one that has much weight still, "Why open up old wounds yet AGAIN and how will that help anything?"

That being said, one of the things I found myself to be at my core is transparent. And like the women of the Kibera training, I have to choose by my thoughts and actions whether to be transparent or not. So even though my immediate reaction is to hide behind the silence of not sharing, like you my choice of actions and subsequent behavior is the essence of who I am in the real world. This brings me back to the African saying and my wish to truly exist in this universe. I will by my thoughts and actions be to the best of my abilities who I was created to be and as such, I will truly exist in the universe.

So I decided to share some of the more personal and difficult experiences of my life with them, as I am with you through these letters. I have discovered, by the way, that by voicing our weaknesses and challenging moments to others it is not a sign of weakness at all. It is a very powerful process where in the end one can own them, and once owned they no longer have the negative impact or hold upon us each day as they previously enjoyed. One does not need to hide anymore and that too is a part of being empowered.

So you see we each have our own challenging journey to take when we go within to find our answers. The experience of the 80 women from Kibera was a life changer for me as I know it was for many of them. For me it was as if all I had struggled and fought through to simply survive had been for this moment and experience. All of the struggles within my life combined with all of the experiences and learning were now merging with my spirit's influence as to who I was and where I was going... and I felt an inner joy and peace of spirit I had seldom felt at any time in my life.

It was as if by my working hard to put what I had experienced and learned together with the deeper knowledge of my spirit, I would finally have the ability to help people change their reality from one of sadness, meaninglessness and despair into lives full of meaning, happiness, hope and passion. I was home in terms of where I needed to be and I knew then why my spirit had so forcefully encouraged me to take that leap of faith and come to Kenya.

And yet how could I possibly help people back home understand any of this? I was just getting it all figured out for myself let alone making it understandable and clear to the two of you, to your mom – or to *my* mom and sisters for that matter!

So my intended five-week stay in Kenya turned into five months and as my visa was about to expire, I finally needed to return home. I knew in my heart I was going to return to Kenya to see if I could build through Women for Justice in Africa the kind of empowerment and self-leadership program I envisioned. I also knew that funding my return would be a problem. I also knew I needed to take some time and make sure I was still thinking clearly. It was time to come home to reflect a bit.

More when I can.
Dad

Hellen (L) and Mary Okioma – Part of my new family in Kenya.

Rajmohan Gandhi's Initiatives of Change Team. From R-L Steve Kimaru, Dr. Gandhi, Mrs. Gandhi, Ann Njeri **(left-side 1st row) and myself 2nd from left in 2nd row.**

It is amazing how hard people work to survive each day within a Kenyan slum area.

Ruth and I at the Initiatives of Change Conference and Training Center in Panchgani, India.

Ruth and I with Rhea D'Souza (behind with hand on my shoulder) and International Interns at the Initiatives of Change Centre in Panchgani, India.

A small group of the women from the Kibera slum within the empowerment and self-leadership training.

February 2, 2014

Dear David and Matt

I hope you know how proud I am of the two of you. Of course, most dads are proud of their sons and daughters but I am also proud each of you has a sense of compassion for people and a willingness to serve people no matter who or where they may have come from. It is a trait we need to help more young people learn – the traits of tolerance and acceptance. I say young people as I have almost given up on many of the adults in this regard – almost but not quite! And in regard to the youth of the world, there are so many that if we cannot get to them soon in terms of learning how to think differently and aligning of actions and thoughts with values and purpose, I cringe to think of what kind of adults they will make and what they will create. We just can't afford more of the same I sense...

I think older people get locked into their experiences and learning to such a degree they are not as inquisitive as they once were. They are still inquisitive to some degree yet have created the reality that with all their experiences and knowledge they now just *know*! After all, how could they have achieved such a position of authority unless they were doing something right?

Perhaps I should go into some detail as to why there is such a need to understand the way we think and create reality so we can learn *how* to think differently. For as long as we continue to think in the same manner, we will not be able to meet and conquer the huge challenges facing societies, people and cultures around the world today. We will continue to react and repeat the past instead of responding and creating a new present and future.

I have come to realize just how complicated, and at the same time how simplistic, our minds truly are. A paradox to be sure (as most things in the universe are) yet what our minds do is pretty simple although how it does it is a series of complicated events scientists are still attempting to unravel.

Here is the simplistic part. Everything I see, hear, touch, smell, sense or otherwise comprehend is stored as a memory within the vast data storage bank of my mind. I have no idea how many terabytes of memory it can hold or even if there is an upward limit to its storage capacity. Yet whether there is a set limit on what we can know is not relevant as most of us as have such a *huge* amount of unused storage capacity within our minds. Consequently, learning and storing new ideas and concepts is perhaps a problem of will but certainly is not an issue of capacity!

That being said, with each bit of information stored within our minds, there will be an emotion attached to it so that when a bit of information is recalled, an individual will sense the emotion first with the actual information coming a bit later. For example, an individual may have been bitten badly by a dog at one point in their life and of course it was a very scary and painful experience. Because of that experience, each time they see a dog, the first thing they may sense is fear or caution or perhaps a sense of apprehension – the emotion of the memory. After the situation is over and someone asks them why they seemed so nervous around the dog, the facts of the event (the memory) will come out. Perhaps as some suggest it is our biological way of protecting ourselves from veering into harm's way: feel the emotion, react, escape and figure out why later.

If we look at the above example a bit deeper, all of the experiences of our lives to date, all we have been taught and all we have otherwise learned consciously or subconsciously over time have been stored in our mind's mega-gig flash drive along with corresponding emotions. It is from that memory base or from our "meter of memory" we interpret what it is we are experiencing – our reality if you will.

Let me give another example. When I see something, say a giraffe, I really do not see anything of the sort per se. What I technically see are photons being reflected, of which my amazing eyes pick up and transmit through the lens, retina, optic nerve and some other neat little doodads until the "photon code" reaches my mind. My mind will immediately begin to search its storage bank of memories to find the best match it can, upon which I will recognize it as an animal and perhaps even the name giraffe.

Of course the emotion will come first and I might behave with joy, fear, glee or curiosity depending upon what was matched to what I had previously learned or experienced. And where I may find excitement and joy upon being surprised by the appearance of such a large object, someone else might be frightened by the shock of something so large coming their way – again, depending upon the match within their memory from the knowledge they have gained up to that point.

Of course it is possible one's mind cannot find a match as there simply was nothing cataloged in memory that can be matched due to a lack of experience, learning or education. In such cases the individual may be baffled having no idea what it is. It is possible they may not see it at all; that is to say the eyes will pick up the photons being reflected but since the mind cannot match it with anything, there may not be a conscious awareness it is even there. As science has discovered, we see much more than we are aware of.

This is not unusual and it happens to us all of the time. How many times for example has someone tried to point something out to you and you simply could not see what they were alluding to? Then, upon getting more information such as, "Do you see the tallest tree directly ahead of you? Now take your fist and go up three fist lengths and look for a black thing that seems to be waving around in the sky. Now do you see it?" And of course you will.

Yet the fact is your eyes already saw it the first time but your brain could not match it as it was wildly trying to find something it could not match. It probably didn't help when they simply said, "Holy shit, would you look at that!"

Your mother was like that sometimes when we were in the car. I would be driving and all of a sudden there would be a terrible shout of alarm, "Look out!!!!" My mind knew something was out there that was alarming and potentially dangerous but I did not have enough information to match with her shout of alarm. Was it ahead or behind us? Was it another car? Was it an animal about to run into us or a missed sign for the correct turnoff? Was it an alien death ray taking retribution for our keeping their friends in Area 51? WHAT?!

After the near heart attack was over and my adrenaline backed off survival mode, I politely (I'm sure it was politely) suggested it would be really helpful if she would provide just a bit more information such as,

"Look out for that car turning in front of us or look out for the alien death ray off to your left!"

The point being, without that added information, my mind simply had nothing to match the warning with and thus I saw nothing much, to the shock of your mother. With more information, I could match it with what I knew, see it and react to it immediately.

Now to be fair, I too have been guilty of giving inadequate information. Your mother and I were flying in our small PA 24/250 Piper Comanche and I was making a night NDB approach to a small airport in rural Nebraska. As you recall, an NDB (Non-directional Beacon) approach is the use of instruments only to get lined up with a runway, with this type of approach not being as accurate as say the ILS approach used at larger airports.

Anyway, a storm was coming and being I was the pilot, I really wanted to land the first time knowing a missed approach might make it so we were landing about the same time the wind and rain hit the airport.

I was working hard on the flight controls as the winds were tricky and at one point it appeared I would not be able to land and would have to go around and try it again. Unfortunately for Jan I began thinking out loud and said, "Shit, we're not going to make it." Of course her mind was able to match that phrase easily and she shouted in alarm, "Are we going to crash?!"

By that time I had managed to get on the correct flight path and we landed a couple of minutes later when I had to apologize for scaring her. I had said aloud what I was thinking. Had I stated I was not going to be able to land this time and would have to go around for another attempt it would have been much clearer to her. She reminded me (I'm sure politely) that it would have been very helpful if I had added that other bit of information so her life would not have flashed before her eyes a few moments ago. It was a fair point.

Another example of how this works is an experience with you David. We were at the airport when four World War II aircraft flew low overhead packed closely together. When I saw it, my mind matched it, and with a sense of glee I said, "Look David, they are flying in formation!"

Your mind had not seen or learned anything about planes flying closely together so you formed your own new mindset to be matched at a later time. The next day that chance came when two planes were flying closely together overhead to which your brain matched it with what you had learned the day before, thus your saying, "Look Dad, there is a 'two-mation!" In short, your mind matched my word "formation" with the fact that there were actually four planes. So to you it was only logical for two planes flying closely together to be a two-mation! And in your reality, it was!

For you, Matt, do you remember the times we would be in a more heated discussion and you would finally in total exasperation say something to the effect, "I'm not going to say anything more, Dad, as you just don't understand… no offence intended." And though it is not easy for me to admit this to you, Matt, you were right. For what you were saying to me matched perfectly what you had seen, experienced and learned to date in your life. However, when I heard your words I immediately matched them with MY experiences and learning up to that point and in fact there was virtually little chance the two realities from our individual experiences and memories would match very well. We think we understand perfectly what the other is saying but it is usually an illusion.

This is why I teach people who are having "communication issues" to stop and do one of two things. If speaking to someone, stop and ask, "Now tell me what you heard me say." If one is listening to another stop them and say, "Let me stop you for a moment and tell you what it is I'm hearing you say." You will be astonished how many times either approach will show that neither person was on or near the same page. Sometimes people are not even in the same book based upon what their minds have matched the words, tone of voice, body language etc. with!

The above is what most of us do. We match things with what we know and react to that emotion-packed memory. Others will then react to our reaction creating different realities which are mostly incompatible. No wonder communicating is still the number one problem cited by HR executives, groups, organizations, families, couples and nations!

Let me use one last example. Let's say a woman I will name Lucy has been taught, has otherwise learned or experienced things indicating to her all men are scumbags. In her mind, men lie, cheat, and say anything to get what they want and once obtaining it throw it away as if it had little value after that.

With such a batch of stored memories it should not be surprising how Lucy will react to a handsome stranger approaching her with a smile asking if she would be willing to have a cup of coffee. Now truth be told, this guy is really her knight in shining armor, the man she has been praying to meet someday. Yet her first reaction was of mistrust, perhaps anger or a sense of being uncomfortable.

Naturally, her answer to the friendly gesture was "no" with perhaps a tone of voice or body language indicating the emotion that was linked to the memories of why all men are scumbags in her reality. In other words it was a, "Perhaps when Hell freezes over" kind of a no. Please note that whenever we react and repeat actions, we close off the possibilities of what could be for our lives and future. In this case her knight in shining armor became just another scumbag.

In short, far too many people react automatically to what they have experienced, been taught or otherwise learned consistent to the memory/emotion stored and then matched by their minds. *In that sense most people, including you and me, are constantly repeating their past while believing they are freely choosing and acting on their own.*

They are not.

It is with this in mind we must ask ourselves what it is we have learned or experienced in our own lives in order to fully understand the lens through which we are seeing the world around us (our world view). We must become aware of what is truly behind our world view to better understand why we react and think the way we do. For not only do we react the same way when a particular match is found, we do it each time that match is brought up in our mind's own internal Google search of "what is that?"

On a broader scale, what if people have been taught, have experienced or otherwise learned that a certain group, culture or tribe is bad, corrupt or evil? In the United States perhaps that would explain the mistrust and near hatred many conservatives and liberals reserve for the other. In the Middle East it would explain the mindsets many Palestinians and Israelis have for one another. In religion it would be what fundamental Christians and Muslims think of each other while in parts of Africa why tribes react so violently toward one another such as the various attempts at genocide and on a smaller scale the post-election violence in Kenya in 2007/2008.

In far too many cases, and granted this is taking a broad brush to make a point, the memory along with the emotions of terror, anger, revenge, pain and fear attached will not only create the reality of how people or groups see each other but also set the foundation for the reaction and consequent behavior and actions each will consistently take upon the other with each new circumstance.

What we have been taught, all our experiences and what we have otherwise learned throughout our lives is the prison which too many people in the world find themselves trapped within. We take information from each of our senses, match it and react thus repeating the behavior each time the same match is found, making each day seem just like the day before.

I say prison for that is exactly what it is. Millions of people, perhaps billions, are trapped to the point where they are constantly repeating their past while not aware they are doing so. They think they are in control of both their thinking and behavior when in fact they are not. They are simply reacting to past memories and emotions every time.

I think it is probable that to most people around the world, just the mentioning of two words – President Obama – will strike an immediate memory/emotion/

reaction in their minds. I suspect neither of you will have the same reaction to the President but you will have a reaction! There seems to be very little middle ground as Americans in particular seem to be in the hate him, love him or are disappointed camps. You may find the same kind of memory match/reactions within your own mindsets with some of these words too:

- Liberals
- Apartheid
- Republicans
- Nelson Mandela
- Idi Amin
- Capitalism
- Socialism
- Snakes
- Drones
- China
- Gun control
- Death penalty
- Paraguay
- Homosexuality
- Politicians
- Africans
- Cats
- Global warming
- Sex
- Spiders
- Religion
- Police
- The United States
- Fundamental Muslims
- Fundamental Christians
- Multi-national
- ISIS
- Conservatives

Hopefully you get the idea. And yet, if those who loved President Obama could magically purge all of their information and substitute in its place all the memories and experiences from those who hated President Obama, what do you think their new mindset, reaction and behavior might be? Most likely their memory/

reactions would be completely reversed and they would believe with the same passion and conviction in their new mindset as they did with the old one.

And whether believing in the first or the second mindset after the information swap, they would still firmly believe that they simply "know" this to be true. They would speak, act and behave in a manner suggesting that what they understood to be true was in fact a real Universal Truth. Sadly it is only the illusion made up from what they know and or have experienced.

Clearly what we know dictates to a large degree the realities we see. We could be on one side or the other depending upon the information (experiences) we have had within our lives. This makes what we believe to be true a little less secure doesn't it?

Now here is the kicker. Once we are aware we are prisoners of what we know, it can easily be seen that as prisons go it is an incredibly small one. Let's do a mind experiment to show the point.

Say we were able to take each bit of information we know both consciously and subconsciously and turn each bit into a grain of sand. Then we put it all out there for everyone to see. How big a beach do you think you would have or in this case know? Although people might be afraid to look, I suspect each would be pleasantly surprised how big their beach was. We actually know a lot… at least so it seems at first blush.

Now let's speculate a bit and do the same thing for all of the bits of information we do not know in the vast universe and turn each of those into grains of sand. After putting it out there to see, how far would that beach stretch? If yours is anywhere close to mine, it would seem almost infinite in length. What I do not know is indeed staggering even to my robust imagination!

Yet one of the important things in beginning to understanding how we think is *what we conclude* after comparing what we know to what we do not know. And like I stated earlier and using me as an example, what I know looks more like the size of an atom compared to what I do not know.

The point being that when one thinks about the magnitude of what they do not know it is then possible to understand that much of what we think we know as truth is probably not even close. This will be hard for many to accept as it brings in confusion and uncertainty where before had been nothing but clarity and certainty.

One only has to go back in time where many learned people at various times strongly believed certain things to be true. Many in fact fought and died defending or challenging those beliefs and some are still believed today. Here are some examples:

- The world was flat. (As an aside, whether they are correct or not, I smile when I hear leading scientists of today state that more and more it looks like the universe is pretty flat!)
- The earth was the center of the universe.

- The bubonic plague was caused by the wrath of God.
- When sick, a person should be bled to get the toxins out.
- There is only one way to get to heaven.
- The sound barrier could not be broken.
- Slavery is acceptable.
- Killing a Saracen or Infidel was not murder but the pathway to heaven.
- Women with white hair are witches.
- Time is always constant.
- God is on our side.
- Samaritans, lepers, prostitutes and tax collectors are unclean and should be avoided.
- People are incapable of governing themselves.
- Democracy is evil and must be stopped at all costs.
- Natural disasters such as the one that hit Haiti are God's wrath unleashed upon them for immoral behavior.

Of course, many of us today look back and shake our heads marveling how people could believe such things to be true. Then again, would anyone really be surprised to learn the people on earth 500 years into our future will be laughing at the silly, superstitious and idiotic things we deeply believe to be true?

So let's look at what we have so far. One: as people we are mostly reactors and repeaters in our thinking and behavior which is aligned directly to the memories/emotions that have been stored within the mind (mindsets) and two: the sum of what we know (or think we know) is incredibly small when compared to what we do not know.

This explains in many ways why so many believe people cannot change as they see the same repeating behaviors from either themselves or others day after day, year after year. *This also explains why so many people around the planet are controlled by others so easily.* For once one understands that people react and behave from what they know, it is only necessary to control what people know in order to get them to behave in the way those in positions of authority desire.

Now I could use the United States for my example here but to give you a more worldly look let me use Kenya even though I could use most other nations as well.

In Kenya I am constantly amazed at the control tribal Elders and others in positions of authority have in controlling the people within their tribe as to whom they should vote for in national, regional and area elections. They understand how to use the prevailing mindsets they have helped perpetuate by evoking standard phrases and concepts used around the world such as, "If we do not vote for our 'own people' we will get nothing for surely if the other side wins, they will take all they can leaving us out in the cold."

And yet, for over 50 years since independence Kenyans have followed the advice of their Elders or party leaders only to find far too many of those being elected becoming rich, creating one of the most corrupt systems in the world while the economic plight of an increasing majority of Kenyans remains dire with most in survival mode. Even today about half of Kenya's 47 million people live on about $1 (USD) a day. Yet, even with this ever continuing reality, Kenyans still vote for the same sort of people or those chosen by the people in positions of authority!

Does this sound familiar to anyone elsewhere in the world? Does it sound similar to some of the discussions the three of us had about Americans being upset about their government yet continuing to vote the same people or same kind of people back into political office? For even in our country, there is an ever increasing gap between the haves and the have nots, the number of poor is increasing, infrastructure is in terrible need of repair, education is slipping in many ways, debt is increasing, we have been at war for the past 10 or more years and we still give healthy tax breaks to the rich. And in spite of people on both the left and the right complaining, we still elect the same kind of people as we did before to lead us.

We have seen this phenomenon over and over again throughout history in terms of cultures, societies, governments and religions. It is sad to see the millions of people actually being controlled so easily and the degree to which they believe they are not. Yet such are the mindsets that have been created and the plight billions around the world find themselves in. And they will continue to be in that plight until they begin to understand how to break out of their self-created prisons by learning how to change from simply being reactors and repeaters to becoming responders and creators of new realities and possibilities for their lives.

Of course, it is also easy to understand why those in positions of authority today view such things as the people learning to think differently in ways that truly empower them as a dangerous, potentially subversive act. From their viewpoint, once people begin to respond rather than react, they will change what they think and do and many of those holding positions of authority will find themselves out in the cold if not worse.

A good example was the reaction members within the Government of Kenya under then President Kibaki had to USAID programs geared toward the empowerment of the youth and women of Kenya. Charges filled with indignation and anger were launched by various government officials including Members of Parliament that the United States was attempting to overthrow the government of Kenya and the people of Kenya would not stand for such arrogant intrusions and violations of Kenyan national independence!

http://www.the-star.co.ke/news/article-78833/americans-want-overthrow-government

http://roba.the-star.co.ke/news/article-78349/kenyan-youth-are-not-engaged-subversion

In a real sense they were correct although not in the context, way or tone those in Kenyan positions of authority were presenting their arguments.

The truth is, when people begin to think differently in terms of not just reacting to old and current mindsets but responding to create new mindsets and realities, they will act and behave differently. They will be empowered as they realize the power to change everything lies within themselves and not upon others.

It is from that point those in authority will not be able to control people by using mere words to manipulate their previous mindsets anymore. Instead they will actually have to DO something including stopping the corruption and the mass feeding at the trough of the people's treasury. If they do not, then they will be removed, and technically when people vote to elect new people and kick out the old office holders the government has been overthrown. That is what free elections are for – to put the people's stamp of approval or to vote them out and change government leaders in a non-violent way.

To the people's detriment, however, the typical reaction of those in positions of authority to programs empowering people on the ground is to oppose and stop them! That is the reaction many in Kenya's government at the time had. It is also the mindset that many people in positions of authority have in the world today including businesses, organizations, communities, governing bodies, religions, families and couples.

I am reminded of a CEO of a company who had decided not to do a self-leadership and empowerment training for her employees. When asked why, she stated forcefully, "What if by being empowered they all choose to leave?" Of course the perfect response to that mindset is, "What if they were not empowered and they all stayed?"

In reality, what all the leaders in various positions of authority were doing in Kenya was manipulating the mindsets of the people in order to continue their ability to stay in power. And they did so by taking advantage of anti-American and anti-colonial memories that Kenyans have been taught, experienced or otherwise learned throughout their lives. As such they attempted to shut down the American empowerment program for youth and women, thus ensuring that Kenyans would be hindered in their attempts in becoming empowered and learning the power they each have to change that status of their lives.

For in order to change we must learn to think differently and the key foundation for doing so is to understand how to change from being reactors/repeaters to responders and creators.

And the way to thinking differently is to recognize our reactive behaviors, stop them, ask ourselves what is it we truly wish to create, decide the steps needed to make that happen, choose to take those steps and to let go of the past. If we learn to do this, we have shifted our thinking from merely reacting and repeating the past toward responding and creating something new in the present thus creating a new future.

So that is a bit of what I teach and believe.

If I remember correctly, my story left off with my coming back to Nebraska after my first experience of Kenya and her people. I shall start there next letter if that is OK...

love you,
Dad

Teaching business entrepreneurs on learning how to think differently.

March 25, 2014

Dear David and Matt

I spoke of some of what I think about various things last time as I believe it is important that you know or at least have a chance of knowing a bit about your dad and his views. But I promised to start where I had left off on my story and my first trip home after initially going to Kenya.

It is strange, yet I do not remember much about coming back home. I remember not wishing to leave Kenya and yet wanting to come home to see you guys and of course family. I also knew if I were to go back and build my dream there, I would have to settle accounts and free myself so as to be able to return to Kenya. I also needed to find funds to live on when back in Kenya as income revenue would be the bare minimum until work permits and the leadership trainings got going within WOJA or LDG.

Money sources for the road back to Kenya were scarce so once again I began to learn about the "letting go" of stressing about the "how" and simply concentrate on just taking the next step in the direction I needed to go. It was the continuation of my learning about the deeper side of the word faith and the phrase "leap of faith" coming once again front and center.

I was beginning to understand that faith wasn't just a blind belief that everything would turn out the way I wished. Faith was becoming more of a "knowing" I was meant to travel a certain road and whatever happened along that road I would be able to deal with it. And though it is true that the concept of "dealing with it" fits any and all roads traveled, there seemed to be a difference for me as I traveled the path of empowering people and helping them become authentic leaders of self and with others.

The difference was that my spirit was calm and seemed to be pulsing with energy and joy where before I dealt with things but I was not at peace within myself. Faith was becoming for me not a promise that everything to come was going to be as I wished, *but that no matter what came along "I" meaning the core of who I was would be OK and that I would find meaning and joy no matter what circumstances would come my way.*

There is an amazing empowerment with that knowledge, guys. I now knew I could be poor or rich, successful or a failure by any society's standards and my spirit would be strong, alive, free and joyful no matter where I found myself. I knew where I wanted to go and all I needed to do was to take the next step.

As I look at the people who have so changed people and the course of world events, they all knew where they needed to go. I do not believe they had any clue of what would happen or whether they would succeed or not in achieving their dream. I do believe they understood where they needed to go and simply chose to take the next step... then the next. And when knocked down or back a few steps it didn't matter... they would simply take note of where they were, refocus on where they wished to go and take another step.

This is such a critical concept to understand if any of us are going to be happy, my sons. We live in a chaotic universe where good things can happen to bad people and bad things can happen to good people with little or no rationale or reason. So to have success defined as the meeting of one's goals is truly a win/lose scenario and there is no need for those odds.

We can have a win/win scenario no matter what happens if we know where we need to go from deep within our spirit, align the amazing capacity of our minds to that path and simply take the next step. The joy will flow from taking the next step and the knowing that one is indeed becoming and doing what they were created to do. So the joy comes from the steps, the journey if you will, with the outcome not being as important. It also takes away many of the things we have been taught to stress about which also helps in our overall quality of life.

In this way, faith was becoming more tied to my learning to let go of trying to control everything to get the outcomes I wanted. I was learning there was a *huge* difference between trying to manipulate the things around me and organize it all into getting what I wanted compared to taking the next step along my chosen path and responding to whatever came my way, which would obviously become the basis for the next step.

My wanting to control shifted from trying to get others to do what I wished them to do, to my working to control my own thoughts, choices and actions to be who I wanted to be and to take actions taking me to the next step. I was still controlling but controlling what was actually controllable – me – and not trying to control the uncontrollable – the chaotic universe that I was in relationship with.

Let me put that in another perspective. I was learning what I had been taught about controlling the outcomes I desired was complete nonsense, a point which many of today's "leading for success" gurus would argue vociferously against I suspect. I was learning that the universe simply did not function that way in spite of our attempts to make it so.

In the case of my thoughts and actions, they are like waves of infinite possibilities emanating from me outward. As the energy of those thoughts and actions spread they will collide with all of the waves of infinite possibilities emanating from everything I am in relationship with at that moment. It is the interaction of all those waves of possibilities that create the outcome of which my role is only one small piece, albeit an important one.

This is why it does not help to imitate what someone else has done. They did it from the mindsets they had from their own experiences and learning. They took action and developed thoughts around the paths they decided to take which in turn interacted with all of the energies put out by all they were in relationship with at the time creating the outcomes we observed or perhaps read about.

It can never happen that way again even if they came back and did it all over again, for everything around them would have changed as would the outcomes.

This is why so many people and businesses struggle. They are initially successful but, over time, things around them change and as such doing the same things that brought them a sense of success will interact with a different set of potentials and the outcomes will be different. For many, the trained reaction is to simply work harder or to go back to "the basics." Yet the harder they work or the more they get back to the basics, the worse things may get. This is why I think people teaching young entrepreneurs started using the phrase "Work *smarter* not harder!"

I was learning the critical key was not to attempt controlling all that was around me but to become more aware of all that I was in relationship with so as to sense subtle changes and respond to those changes in a way that kept me on the path where I intended to go. People and companies who understand this will be more able to sustain their programs and efforts. They will be able to survive. The same can be said for us.

Coming home gave me the chance to think a bit more about all of this and the actions or next steps I needed to take.

You might recall that I loved to collect old coins and actually at one time considered being a coin dealer. I even created a company I named Commoncents Coins after good ole Thomas Paine's famous writings. Not surprisingly that did not go anywhere... it was not the path I was supposed to take. BUT, my dabbling in that field created the opportunity for funding my next step in my returning to Kenya and it took the intervention of a man who had been a real pain in my side when I was a Senator, Tom Bassett.

He was then retired but years before, when I was a Senator, he was active in lobbying for better health care and such things. If I remember correctly, I had just won my first election much to everyone's amazement and I was acutely aware some of my views were way more liberal than the majority of my constituency.

Thus I felt I should do some things from time to time to establish my conservative roots for future election support. A very stupid, self-serving and short-sighted decision I might add in hindsight, yet at the time I was still attempting to be what I thought I should be rather than to just be myself.

To put a much harsher view to it, I was attempting to manipulate the majority of conservatives into supporting me next election by saying and doing things they would naturally support based upon their own well-established mindsets.

So along came a legislative bill where a large group of respected individuals in positions of authority in the North Platte business community opposed for the reason they might lose the support of a major sponsor for the community's largest celebration if the bill passed. And yet, the bill was actually going to do the right thing: stop the giving of free samples of smokeless tobacco to under-aged youth and in the end, everyone.

Of course the board members were looking at it through their own mindsets of "whatever it takes to make the celebration financially solvent" and not particularly caring about the bigger picture of the problems smoking and particularly smokeless tobacco had on anyone who used the product. They, like I was about to do, found justifications for their actions so that they actually convinced themselves their position was the correct one for their community. It was not.

But I was going to react to what I had experienced and been taught about what being a leader was all about. I was about to support the local leadership for political reasons to help secure re-election in the future and temporarily put my values of doing what was right aside for a while. My mind told me what it had seen and learned: that politics was a tough game and sometimes one had to do something distasteful in order to live another day to fight for something that was right. And besides, I told myself, tobacco was a legal product and adults should have the right to choose for themselves whether to use it or not or whether to take a free sample. After all don't most legal products give out free samples in order to attract new customers?

All of these were thoughts I felt conservatives would like me to stand up for (less government, more freedom type of thing) and so I began the process of justifying my own upcoming actions to be "right." I knew the leaders back home were looking to see what their rookie Senator could do and I was about to show them thus gain their future support!

But the pitfalls, traps and trip wires in politics are lethal in so many ways to the conscience of the spirit, and if one is not well centered and focused on what their core values and purpose are and committed to think and do things that are in alignment with those things, the politician will falter and in the end become one of "them" and part of a system that values profits or personal gain over people.

I didn't even know my core values or purpose at this time so clearly I was in trouble but was oblivious to it all, except deep down I sensed it. I know I did. It was the beginning of my becoming someone I did not wish to be and in the end became a big reason for my resigning eight years later and getting out before I became forever lost.

Anyway, I opposed the bill for "political reasons" and of course came up with a myriad of reasons to justify my actions. In fact, the more I talked about it, the more I actually began to convince myself I actually WAS doing the right thing. But deep down I knew that was not the case. I ignored those feelings, refusing to feed them. Fortunately there were wiser people who did the right thing and the bill passed and of course the sponsor never left in spite of what they had insinuated earlier. They lied.

This brings me back to Tom Bassett. He seemed to be everywhere: on the radio, on television in the newspapers supporting the bill and lambasting those who were opposed to it. He particularly seemed to find joy in focusing on me and in a series of letters to the editor and personal letters to me continued to ask the one question I did not wish to answer: "How could someone who was intelligent, a former National Teacher of the Year finalist and someone who cares for youth oppose a law that will help keep children and later adults from becoming addicted to a tobacco product with a potential horrible cancerous death to follow?"

He was really starting to get under my skin – not because he was arrogant and harsh in his criticism, but because deep down I knew he was right and I did not have the courage to change my position due to the political mindsets I had developed. My mind was reacting to what it knew: that to change positions now after all the pressure would show weakness and a lack of courage to stake out a position to fight for it.

It was a stupid mindset based on poor information and a particular set of experiences, for in the end the only things worth fighting for are those that are in line with one's core values. If one finds oneself going against that current, a correction is not a show of weakness but a sign of wisdom, intelligence and courage. In the end I stayed the course, decided to take my hits and live again but with a stronger base of support for my next election. And the heat continued to be turned up.

It was an old editor of the local paper, Keith Blackledge, who came to my rescue. He wrote an editorial stating that clearly I was on the wrong side of the issue yet people should think of all of the things I had done for the district when making an overall decision to support me or not. And in his opinion I deserved their support in spite of his disappointment in my position on the tobacco bill. In one editorial he gave me hell, forgave, showed support for what I could do for people and gently reminded me of my values and what kind of person I actually wanted to be. Keith became a valued friend whom I learned I could always talk to knowing he would guide or at least gently lead me into seeing what I should do when the choices became difficult. He died years ago but his wisdom, council and friendship I will cherish forever. He taught me a lot.

In the end, I don't think my position or the hits I took had much of an effect in terms of support. In hindsight, those astute in the political process most likely took note that their Senator might do what they wanted, even compromise his values, if it meant their support later. That was not the kind of Senator or person I wanted to be. I worked hard to never do that again much to the frustration and at times anger within the existing political machinery.

As for Tom Bassett, it turned out he went to your Grandmother DJ's Methodist church and during coffee hour when I was home from Kenya, he came up to reintroduce himself in case I had forgotten our spat almost 10 years before. He did not have to worry about my not remembering who he was.

I literally groaned when I saw him sauntering over my way to say hello. I expected a lot of harassing and teasing, but that was not who he was I soon discovered, contrary to my existing mindset about him. Instead what happened helped me continue my leadership journey!

We had a nice talk and discovered we had a mutual interest in coin collecting. I told him I had decided to sell my more valuable pieces to fund my return trip to Kenya but I would have a hard time selling them as they were expensive and only so many people in the region would have both the funds and the desire to buy them.

As it turned out, he believed he knew someone who might have an interest. About a month later Tom brokered a deal and I sold the coins for which he never charged me a fee for his brokerage service or travel to meet with the gentleman. He said he admired what I was trying to do and it was his way of being able to support my efforts.

I guess as I look back I can now see how one of my main antagonists became a major supporter as we shared the same values. It also shows the possibilities are infinite in all relationships and actions as long as we do not become blinded by our previous mindsets formed from past experience.

So the funds were received and along with the added income from my selling everything else I owned in a huge garage sale, I was ready to return to Kenya. I felt I had enough to live on for about 18 months when hopefully permits would be obtained and income would be generated from work in Kenya. And though that thought seemed to make sense from my Nebraskan/American mindsets, it turned out to be incredibly naïve.

I dearly loved my time I was able to spend with the two of you and with my sister Cris and her husband

Ron, "baby sister" Danna and DJ. But I was also anxious to take the next step and so when the day of departure came, I was sad to leave but anxious to go at the same time.

I want to add that because of the impact the women in the Kibera training had on me, I decided I needed to go visit my sister Cris and her husband Ron. I had never taken time to go visit them myself in all the years they had been in Florida. As such we had drifted apart. My stay there was wonderful and the distance that had come between us was no longer there. It is amazing what talking, listening and being with people can do toward keeping relationships alive and healthy.

Perhaps the hardest part of the trip was saying goodbye to Cris. I remember her having tears in her eyes and saying that she was so happy to have her brother back in her life. I felt the same way and left knowing I had a strong family behind me supporting and encouraging me as I found my way along the road I needed to travel.

I had totally committed myself to building an authentic leadership program in the world which I believed was supposed to begin in Kenya. The goal would be to help people learn how to think differently, align their thoughts and actions to core values, determine their purpose and path to be taken, and have the courage to act upon it. I would be building upon the concepts that no one can lead anyone without first learning to lead themselves, leadership that matters comes from the inside out, and how all of these things can create a new reality in the present and thus change the possibilities for the future.

As an aside, I found these concepts would lead me to develop with my colleagues at Effective Change Consultants (ECC) a powerful program on anti-corruption, but that was to come a bit later as I became its CEO.

I had nothing left of value back home except you, family and friends of course. All was gone and there was a sum of money I was taking with me that would not last long as I went to create that dream which had always been within me to make a difference in the world. For many my course of action seemed stupid and unrealistic. Others felt that it was brave and courageous. For me it was all of them *and* it was the next step I needed to take and I knew it. So I took it.

It didn't take long before everything in my life changed. But let me stop for now as I am tired and you probably need a break from reading too.

Love you both so very much!

Dad

Speaking within the Nebraska Legislative Chamber.

A rare moment with siblings all together. **From L-R Cris, myself and Danna.**

April 1, 2014

Dear David and Matt

You know I was just thinking about the two of you and it occurred to me the two of you are the only brothers who individually and separately found a way to vote for a bill in the Nebraska legislature! David, you were the first.

You were sitting with me on the legislative floor watching everything as usual with your unique way of figuring out what was going on. If you recall, on my desk was a series of four buttons all color coded: red for voting "no," green for voting "yes," blue for getting a page (college legislative intern) to help with something, and white to say one wished to speak. Besides "voting" when you weren't supposed to, I especially remember you both liking to push the blue button as college students acting as pages would come and bring you free hot chocolate!

There was an intense discussion going on at the time and if I remember correctly, David, you were seated in my chair while I was engaged in conversation and somewhat distracted. I remember hearing the Clerk of the Legislature say, "All those in favor vote aye, opposed nay" with the sound of the voting bell ringing loudly signaling to all Senators it was time to vote.

As I looked up to see how the vote was going I was shocked to see I had already voted! When I got to you, you looked so proud in your decision to vote for me it was impossible to be angry. In fact Senator Ron Withem, a good friend and mentor, noticed the whole thing and commented that it was the smartest vote I had made all session!

When he asked you how you decided which way to vote you simply stated you looked at the board and it looked like there were more greens than reds and you wanted to be on the winning side! As it turned out, that was the way I was going to vote so nothing needed to be done. Later Senator Withem commented that your voting rationale was possibly better than mine at times! He was teasing of course... I think.

A couple of years later you, Matt, did the same thing but I almost got into trouble for that one. Once again a son of mine was at my seat while I was chatting with other Senators when the vote bell clanged and once again the Clerk of the Legislature Patrick O'Donnell saw

I was not at my desk and immediately understood how I had managed to push my voting button from so far away. He knew from experience a son of mine had just "voted" which of course was in violation of countless rules within the legislature. Yet once again you, like David, voted as I would have giving my friends fodder for teasing for years whenever I complained about the stress and pressures that came with the voting at times. They would simply say, "It can't be that bad... even a five-year-old can do what you do!"

I sometimes wonder the impact my being a Senator had on the two of you. Perhaps for you it was "normal" as that was just the way it was. It was anything but normal I'm afraid. I wonder how many fathers and their sons carry on a lively discussion debating the values of capitalism, democracy, socialism and communism while in the car driving home from the state Capitol to our home in North Platte?! I also remember other discussions on income distribution between the rich and the poor, drug policies and of course American military policies, and the time seemed to fly as we drove the few hours home.

I also remember the pride I had of your awareness of things and the issues that impact so many people around the world. Even then the two of you had a passion for not accepting the norm simply because it was the accepted thing to think or do. You also had compassion for people that I knew would serve the two of you well in your futures no matter which paths you decided to take.

But those are memories of days gone by.

Today in Kenya I admit to it being hard as a particularly tough "low cycle" has paid me a visit. When I came to Kenya, I decided to wean myself from all medications that were intended to help my depression periods as I was uncertain I would be able to get the meds consistently in Kenya. That and the possibility of having to stop cold turkey was not advisable – something I found out the hard way prior to coming to Kenya!

It is interesting that without the meds, my lows can be pretty deep and yet the things I have learned these past few years have helped me deal with them more than the meds ever could. I now know the lows will pass and the dark lens I see the world through is not as dark as it appears and is mostly illusion. I have also learned when I feel hope seems far away I just need to go back to thinking about why I came to Kenya in the first place and what it is that when I do it gives me so much joy and meaning. Going back to that "why" or the reason I want to take another step has been so helpful over these past years overcoming the low periods. And of course friends from Jamaica and elsewhere will always be with me to carry the day when needed.

In a way it is similar to what I teach others here in learning how to think differently. I first say it is important to recognize what it is one is thinking (rather than just reacting without thinking), then ask what it is one really wants, decide what needs to be done to make that happen, then choose to act while letting go of the previous thinking and/or actions. That and never being afraid to ask for help for none of us can do it alone.

This is why it is important for each of us to find our purpose... or that which we do that gives our life meaning and a deep sense of fulfillment. It is the essence of our being here on earth and it is where one can find the power and strength to take another step or, in the case of a low cycle, to endure another day.

It is a shift of awareness and of thinking perhaps. Where thoughts of depression may cause someone to react more to what is going on around them, thinking and acting from one's purpose and sense of core values will invariably shift the focus toward responding and creating the way they want the experiences of life to be. That difference between reacting and repeating to responding and creating can be everything at times.

So where was I? Oh yes, I was returning to Kenya to build a dream but not before stopping in Yaoundé, Cameroon to be a guest speaker at an International Leadership Conference. It would be there I would learn more of Africa being a place where things are not always as they seem.

The people I met in Yaoundé were wonderful, intelligent and truly working hard to make a difference in the lives of the people of Cameroon, West Africa and Africa as a whole. They had a big dream of forming an international conference and of bringing in some of the top speakers from around the world to work with and teach the over 5,000 people they expected to come on how to become more effective leaders.

They were also about to learn a hard truth: just because one has a great attitude and is committed to working hard, dreams are not that easily created.

Their list of 20 expected international speakers ended up being just five and of the 5,000 expected to pay their registration fee, approximately 200 actually showed up. Of course, without the expected income from the 5,000, they were in financial trouble and would not be able to keep their financial commitments to any of us who managed to make our way there.

Yet it was a very valuable experience and I am glad to have been part of what they were trying to create. Almost everyone I met from Cameroon was poor yet all were doing something to change their lives and those around them. Where they needed further education but had no funds to attend, they found a way. Where they needed to take what they had learned to people in rural Cameroon but lacked the necessary funds to do so, they found a way. And though they felt terrible about not being able to meet their obligations to me, what I saw were individuals daring to dream and willing to take risks to break free from the clutches of poverty and the damage it had caused throughout their lives and their families for generations.

On the down side of visiting Cameroon, instead of returning to Kenya with more money in the bank from the conference as planned, I was going to arrive more in debt. It was not what I had planned but certainly was in line with my knowing my time in Kenya would include experiencing poverty on a more personal level! It was from that point onward that finances became a real challenge in Kenya, more so than even the difficult times back in Nebraska prior to my coming here.

My return to Kenya turned out to be more challenging and frustrating than I had imagined it would be. I tried to create the leadership program through Women for Justice in Africa, yet nothing was coming easily including getting the work permits I needed to earn an income. It seemed every step I chose to take was blocked or otherwise made impassable. It seemed as if I was going nowhere fast.

I was learning to do what I taught others to do – that when the way is shut, one can either quit or take another step. I always seemed to find a way to take that next step as I tried to build something that would impact thousands if not millions of people over time. Yet it felt as if I was stepping in a thick mud with each step getting so mired it took enormous energy to free it only to get stuck once again with the next step. It was as if Kenya and the world around me was pushing back the harder I tried to impact people and change the way things were here and around the world.

Yet while the actual building of the leadership program was painfully slow in developing, there were other aspects of my being here developing quickly, particularly my ability to speak to small groups of people around Kenya. In doing so I was becoming more aware of the real Kenya not just the one tourists and other visitors see. I was getting more into the inner parts of the Kibera slum and into rural Kenya well off the beaten safari paths.

I was beginning to learn more about the people themselves, their culture, tribal differences, and the real meaning and extent of poverty in Kenya and I suspect Africa in general. I was also learning about how many Kenyans view people from countries like the United States and especially Mzungus.

In doing so I discovered what I *thought* I was seeing and my *understanding* of it was in most cases far from what was really happening and why. I began to understand further my need to wipe away all I had been taught and to view things from a "blank slate." I would begin to fill in the blank slate by being curious and asking questions as to what was happening and why. For only by seeing and experiencing what was happening around me in this manner would I be able to see more clearly and experience the richness of the culture around me.

When I tried to put what I experienced into the contexts of my own learning and mindsets, too often what I matched it with simply was not helpful or far off the mark. I couldn't learn about Kenyans or Kenya through my Nebraskan/American eyes and mind. I had to lose that at times to see things through eyes unbiased by my previous learning to begin having a clearer understanding of what was truly going on around me.

I also had to put judgment totally aside for it had the capacity to cloud and confuse everything. Of course, saying this and doing it were and are two totally different things. I can't say I am perfect at having the blank slate and suspending my judgment, yet I am getting better each day as I constantly work at it. If you remember, David, this was the one bit of advice I really emphasized to you and Sarah when you came to visit: come and see from a blank slate, accept things for what they are and judge later if you feel a need to.

For once we begin to judge we are no longer within the reality of what is being experienced or observed. When judging, we retreat into our minds where we are all trapped by what we know. And when we think of what we know compared to what we do not know in the universe, our minds become the prison from which the possibilities of what we could see drops from being infinite into only the one: what our minds have seen and judged to be real and all which will come from that. And from there, change, tolerance, mutual discovery and understanding become nearly impossible.

I think some of the hardest things for me in dealing with having a blank slate and throwing judgment out the door were the Kenyan sense of time, the overriding view that all Mzungus were rich, the ruse of becoming "friends" only to ask for money or support later then dropping all pretense of being friends if nothing was given, and the level of corruption that exists at all levels of society.

My first experience with "Kenyan Time" was in my first workshop for the 80 women of Kibera. The training was supposed to start at 8:30 sharp with all being asked to "keep time." The vast majority did not show up until around 10:00. Of course, I at first stressed about no one showing up and all the planning and donations being for nothing. Then I began to get into a nice "snit" about the program being planned down to the minute and now it was all in a shambles as the first morning was almost gone and we had not even started yet!

Little did I know the true extent of the learning curve I would need to overcome. My education would continue as the day began to unfold.

Most of the women came around 10:00 to 10:30 but there was a scattering of those who came about one every hour throughout most of the day. Yet, instead of sneaking in quietly so as not to disturb anything due to their late entrance, they would all immediately begin to greet everyone within the room. This greeting is not just a quick wave and a smile or a slight nod of the head to all, nosiree! The Kenyan greeting is to go to each individual and go through a shaking hands routine regardless of how many were in the room or how long it took.

I quickly learned that this greeting is a necessary part of Kenyan culture. When another woman came in late and I was in a particularly sensitive part of the training, I asked her to sit down quietly for now and I would catch her up later. The rest of the group just looked at me with shocked expressions on their faces with one finally blurting out, "NO! We must greet them!" And they proceeded to do just that.

From what I have observed, the types of greetings vary. In many parts of the Rift Valley for example, women will tap each other on the left shoulder with their right hand then bring their right hand to the other's with force so there is a "slapping" sound, all the while maintaining contact and shaking hands.

Men have their own routines. One in particular is the slapping of hands together, holding on to the hand to continue the shaking hands part while one "bumps" first the left shoulders together and then the right. My favorite is the slapping of the hands, with the sliding of the hands down to where each clasps the fingers of the other while putting the thumbs together in a snapping type motion.

Of course, then there is the more traditional cross-gender greeting where one simply shakes the hand of the other, then grip the hands a second way with thumbs of each right hand together with fingers wrapped around the hand of the other followed by another hand shake. This may be repeated often... I have yet to figure out how many times are appropriate.

Over time I began to really appreciate the Kenyan concept of greeting each other. From my perspective as an American, it was a waste of valuable time as well as being inconsiderate of the trainer or the program being done at the time. Now I think differently. It is important to see people as people and to interact with them in a personal way. The Kenyan way is very personal where ours is more efficient but impersonal.

So as with so many things, I had to find a way of changing my mindset towards this new time-consuming greeting.

It took a while but all is well now. I had to change my mindset or perception of how things should be from being "efficient" to that of taking time to actually meet people. I had to slow down my sense of time if you will in order to create stronger, more lasting relationships.

I now know it is something we Americans need to do more of. We need to slow down to see people and to build relationships with no intention of getting something later but just to build it for the relationship only.

This also relates in my opinion to the Kenyan concept of time which is surprisingly similar to the concept of time held by the Native American Indians of the Plains. The Lakota Sioux come readily to mind. Their tradition was and is to enjoy each moment for what it is and never be enslaved by things such as time. To them, time was a task master who demanded servitude and they were not about to be slaves to anyone or anything if they had a choice.

I remember once with the Chamber of Commerce we had contracted with a couple of Native American dancing/drum groups to perform at a dedication ceremony. By agreement they would arrive the night before and attend a brief organizational meeting for the next morning's ceremony. By midnight they had not shown and we were way beyond the panic stage by then. We had paid them in advance so they would have money for fuel to come and you can imagine all the various scenarios we were making up on their not showing and no one being able to contact them.

They finally arrived between 4:00 and 6:00 the morning of the show all the while looking at us with bemused looks as we spoke of our panic and concern for them. From their point of view, they had said they would come and perform at the ceremony and they were true to their word. They were honest, thoughtful and incredibly good performers who just were not going to follow our concept of time and how people should live by it.

If the Kenyan greeting is to take a moment to "see" everyone who is there and to build relationships, the sense of Kenyan time to me is similar in concept. To jump a bit into the future in terms of my journey, I will use Ruth who would later become my wife as an example. I would ask her what time in the morning we were to meet with a particular group or be at a certain school to speak. She would tell me politely the agreed upon time was 10:00 in the morning.

For me a 10am meeting created the following scenario: It would take us about 30 minutes to walk there, say 10 to 15 minutes to meet the group leaders and get a sense of the room or area to be used. With that in mind, we would need to leave the house by 9:15 at the latest, say 9:00 just to give us some leeway. I had everything planned according to time and slowly I began to become aware my whole sense of existence was closely related to my sense of time and what needed to be done in the time remaining. The phrase "Times awasting and daylight's aburnin!" kept popping into my mind.

Well, as on most mornings, people dropped by to greet us and many had some issue or problem they wished to talk to Ruth or me about. When company arrives it is Kenyan custom to offer them something which in most cases might mean a cup of tea or some breakfast or a chapatti (think flour tortilla). Some might come unannounced at 7:00 in the morning, others at 9:00 and others... well you get the idea. I tried to be polite but when 9:15 came and went, then 9:30, then 10:00 and we were still at the house greeting and sharing with our uninvited guests, I was literally seething inside.

I remember quietly sneaking Ruth aside and saying something like, "We are SOOO late!! We need to tell these people (note the words 'these people') they have to go as we have things we need to do. Besides they did not tell us they were coming so they should not expect us to change all of what we are obligated to do just because they decided to drop by!"

I was such an American.

Ruth would always say patiently, "Yes, but they are our guests and we need to greet and take care of them. Don't worry, all will be fine." I tried to calm down, but all I could think about were the people expecting me to speak to them, now sitting there waiting with all of their own plans now shot to hell due to our being so late to arrive! I even pictured them getting up and leaving thinking we had forgotten and were not coming.

From my perspective I hid my frustrations well from our guests and was at least in the far corners of my mind the ultimate diplomat. In hindsight I think I probably seemed quite rude from their point of view.

However, please note an important difference in how I was seeing the people visiting our home to how Ruth saw them. I saw them as objects (note again my phrase "these people") while Ruth saw them as human beings. This concept will come back again later as people will always think of and treat "objects" differently than they will human beings... always.

Eventually, we would be on our way, yet each time we would arrive late one of two things seemed to happen. Most often, those we were to meet had not yet arrived and we would sit and wait for perhaps another hour before things were ready to start, or they were not ready to begin yet as they were involved with something else at the time, being totally unconcerned about the time of our arrival. Whichever one was the actual result, we in reality were never late and all my stressing only served to create a negative reality of which I was the only participant.

Eventually I learned another valuable lesson. From my mindset I had assumed if I arrived late, everyone would be looking at their watches and wondering why I was so late and whether they should just leave or stay. That was a false assumption. Everyone simply did what needed to be done and while waiting talked with one another and/or generally enjoyed the moment. They were also truly glad when I arrived, with no sense of being frustrated by my tardiness. I have really tried to learn how to do that as it is a wonderful state of mind to have.

Ruth had such patience for this strange American's thinking! It was as if she knew in time I would figure it out and understand that time wasn't the important factor – people were. Plus, from her point of view, everything would actually turn out OK so there really was no reason to stress. She was right.

I believe that is one of the biggest lessons Kenyans have taught me: people and relationships are more important than time. Perhaps time has a place, yet the basing of what we do, when and how all on time is not what a good life is all about. In fact in many ways I have learned that my concept of time was actually harmful to the actual quality of my life.

Someone once told me that we make thousands of choices each day and when the combination of our choices brings us together, then that is the time we were meant to meet. It cannot always be "scheduled" and each encounter must be seen as the miracle of choices that have made it possible for that moment to exist. We need to recognize the miracle of those moments and take time to be a part of those moments as best we can.

And though I might argue for Kenya to take the leap economically along with the other changes Kenyans say they desire, a bit more timeliness on their part would be very helpful in bringing those changes about. That being said, our servitude toward time is too far on the other side of the pendulum and we need to learn to chill out more and enjoy the moments and the people within them more. I think now if we are to err on one side or the other, we should err on the side of people and enjoying the moments more.

Let me stop here for now as I need to take a break and enjoy some moments for a while!

Love,
Dad

Coming home for my mother's 90th Birthday celebration.

It's a different world when I am back home. Here I am doing an interview with Nebraska Public Television on my work in Kenya.

Speaking at the International Leadership Conference in Yaoundé, Cameroon.

May 15, 2014

Dear David and Matt

It is early May and the rains have finally come to Kenya. They arrived late which has been a concern for those in agriculture. Not so different from farmers in Nebraska who look to the sky for the life-giving rains yet at the same time praying for just the right amount and to avoid the severe weather that can come with it. In Kenya, like elsewhere, there is also concern about global warming, the changing weather patterns and whether the rains will continue to come when needed. This sounds like I know a lot about agriculture... of course the two of you know differently!

I remember one day being on your Grandpa Jess's farm trying to fit in the conversation with a group of neighboring farmers. As you know, my knowledge about farming was and still is pretty limited yet I felt safe enough to say that it was good we received rain the other day. To wit the person next to me said loudly,

"Hell Dave, what use is a small rain when the subsoil moisture is still about zero? Nothing will grow with that!" So I learned about subsoil moisture. The next time I would be a bit smarter!

So the next time came a few years later. Same scenario as before as there was a group of farmers standing in a close circle chatting about the weather. It had been raining cats and dogs (hippos and elephants here in Kenya) so I said with confidence something about all the rain helping the subsoil moisture levels so that things will grow well. I still remember what came next: "Hell Dave, what use is all that subsoil moisture if it is too damn muddy to get into the fields to plant a crop?!"

It was then an epiphany struck me. To be a farmer one needed to be a scientist, a chemist, a marketer, a gambler, a weatherman, feel blessed for what blessings one may have, hope for the best, assume the worst, understand the paradox of all things, see the good in the bad and the bad in the good, then face another day. I think that is the tie that binds farmers all around the world! I have so much admiration for what they do and the circumstances in which they do it.

I remember another time on the farm how excited and shocked everyone was about something I had done. It was no big deal to me, but I actually changed a tire on the tractor I was driving which had broken down in the middle of a field. Everyone was so shocked... imagine!

For me it was a bit embarrassing that people actually felt I did not know how to change a tire. They all had such a mindset of what I could and could not do. It was all very interesting. So I should not have been surprised that Kenyans would also have a particular mindset of what I was like because I was an American and a Mzungu.

I speak not of the elite or the middle class of Kenya, but the vast majority of Kenyans who are poor. From my experience most Kenyans think *every* Mzungu is rich and doesn't work that hard. In fact, we are so rich we simply pay others to do our work for us as we relax. They, like the area farmers thinking of that changed tire, are shocked to see me not only working, but working hard. When I ask some where they learned such things about Americans, all too often I am told, "From your movies!"

And Americans wonder why we are so misunderstood!

℘◊℘

Anyway, back to my story to you. I had returned to Kenya and was becoming more engaged with life in rural Kenya and the plight of the majority of Kenyans within the country. Perhaps now it is time I told you how I met Ruth and why your father at 60 chose to marry a woman from another race and culture with little formal education and who once made her living by brewing illegal alcohol. It is an unlikely story if ever there was one and it eventually led to the best decision I have ever made!

But before I do that, I need to give you a little history about a group of women of which Ruth was a part. This was their (and Ruth's) history before I met them.

Historically women in Kenya (and the world) have had a tough time of it. Sometimes, especially in rural Kenya, women end up having many children but no support as their husbands have taken no responsibility for them or their children. Many find their husbands leaving them as they marry a second or third wife. In far too many cases the women are just abandoned leaving them with no financial support to speak of, few business skills or education to help them. Such was the case for a group of women I encountered one day when doing some leadership workshops in the Central Rift Valley region of Kenya.

The reason these women had little to no formal education was that no one would pay their school fees when they were young. *If* there was money for fees it would go to the boys first. The impact was predictable: the women had few job skills to generate income, little to no family support and all had children needing food, clothing, shelter and future school fees to be paid.

In desperation these women chose to do the only thing making sense given their circumstances: they chose to brew and sell illegal alcohol. It was easy to learn, the demand was high and there was money to help them survive. That was the upside. The downside list got pretty long and in most cases dangerous.

By their own admission, the brewing life was hard but the money could be good at times, not so good other times. Bribes had to be paid to various police officers of the area and those could be expensive. Usually the bribes would be delivered to the police officer's home so that no one at headquarters would know. Even with the bribes there were times when the Area Police Chief cracked down due to pressure from the community to do something.

In such times the women were caught and punished for brewing illegally as they were not warned ahead of time by those they had bribed. A heavy fine usually ensued and all of their pots, pans, and brewing items destroyed meaning a lot of money was again needed to "re-tool." Sometimes they were taken to jail leaving their children behind to fend for themselves and there they would stay until a fine was paid or their sentence served out.

This game of cat and mouse with the police, bribes, getting caught and starting over was their life. In the end, they had little money and their children were not able to go to school. Not to mention having drunk men around or in their homes late at night and all that could mean to a woman with no husband around. Many times men would offer to be their "husband for the night." One woman openly confesses in all honesty not knowing who the father was of some of her children. I liken it to many Americans' experiences in Las Vegas.

They also had to bear a harsh social stigma as they were not accepted in many quarters – even church. First was the knowing that too many people were becoming drunkards and it was hurting society at all levels. Second was the mindset that if there were no brewers the problems of drinking would be vastly reduced, totally ignoring the fact that if the demand was not so high for cheap illegal alcohol there would be few if any brewers. Third was the fear of many a wife that her husband would be stolen by one of those single women brewers. And with polygamy the law of the land, that fear was a very legitimate one.

So the brewers were truly on their own and to fight that, some began to form groups in order to support each other to increase business and to help when things became bad. To that end, 20 women formed a group which they named I'nget Nge'tiet (Ignite the Ignition) Women's Group.

Then one day four of the more elderly brewing women (around 60+ years of age) decided that brewing was not worth it as it harmed so many people and families in so many ways. In their minds there had to be another way. They reasoned if they could each create a small business, they could each make enough to survive without the negativity of what came with illegal brewing, not to mention the social stigma each of them suffered with society around them in general.

At first there was just a lot of "talking" among the 20 women of the group until an unexpected and terrible event changed their talking into acting. The presidential elections at the end of 2007 did not go well.

As the votes were being counted and the nation waited to hear who won, things began to spiral out of control and in the blink of an eye a new president was sworn in quickly in the dead of night before all the votes had been counted.

Soon after that and with explosive force, something happened in Kenya no one had expected or predicted. Violence between Kenyans along tribal lines exploded throughout the country as if someone had poured gasoline on a fire. In the end over 1,000 people were brutally killed and over half a million Kenyans found themselves displaced with nowhere to go as they were chased from their homes or they lost everything as their homes or businesses were burned to the ground. The world and Kenyans everywhere were shocked at the violence which had occurred so swiftly and so unexpectedly.

As the women tell the story they were extremely busy brewing as business was very good – beyond good actually. People were coming and buying large numbers of liters to take away to some get-together or other. The women were happy as money was flowing in.

Then as more people began to drink, the louder the talking became and many customers were overheard speaking about this house or that person who should be burned out or punished. The women did not take much notice of the talk as they had learned long ago that people say stupid things and made a lot of noise when drunk. But over the next few hours stories began to come back indicating this time the talking was not just bluster. The talk had become action and over the next few days all hell broke loose.

The more the women, Kenya and the world began to learn of the post-election violence, the more the women realized the reason their businesses had prospered so much. Quite simply, many of the men and youths were drinking the cheap illegal brew to get the courage to do the terrible things they were planning to do to those they were told were the supporters of those who "stole" the election or to retaliate for the violence that had just occurred to them. Later they would drink even more to celebrate their courageous deeds.

In an instant those who were friends and neighbors the day before were now castigated as "objects" and thus what was once a heart of peace was now a heart of war and the brutality began. As one side attacked the presumed culprits, usually from other tribes, the more those attacked struck back. Their former friends had become objects or one of "those people." Sadly, humanity will always do things to objects they would NEVER do to a human being.

This is why people say such horrible things about people in one political party or individuals serving within governments around the world. They are saying those things to politicians – objects and not human beings.

To say it another way, the best way to bring about violence is to make some individual or group the object of everyone's frustrations and bitterness. Take the humanity out of the equation and people can and will do almost anything. For Americans, just listen to both FOX or MSNBC news and one will see people and groups being objectified every hour. People can be moved to act in terrible ways to that which is an object compared to what one might do to a human being.

As the violence in Kenya subsided and people began to pick up the pieces, the women knew in some ways they had played an indirect role in that violence. It was that moment of truth which pushed the four elderly women to get as many women as they could within the group to stop their brewing and work together as a group to create something different.

Over the next few weeks the elder women of the group tried talking to each group member into changing the group to be one of "non-brewers." It was a tough sell. In the end 16 women of the original 20 agreed to stay with the group and try. Yet they had the same problem everyone in the world has who is poor and needing to start a business: no capital. So after talking, they decided what it was they wanted and more importantly why.

They also understood from past experience no one was going to give them anything. So they made a plan on how to use what little they had to help create 16 new small businesses. What they had was virtually nothing but what they would eventually create would potentially change everything.

I remember once participating in a three-day workshop with my fellow Squirrels in California entitled "Creating from Nothing." That was hard enough but compared to what these women were about to do it was a walk in the park. After all, when our workshop was over we could go back to our nice homes and jobs while life continued as usual. For these women, there was no job or nice home to return to and certainly there were no safety nets for them to land upon if they fell down. It was an all or nothing roll of the dice and to me the courage each of these women showed was simply incredible. It is the courage of the human spirit when it knows what it needs to do and more importantly, why.

Their plan was ingenious and simple as they leveraged what little they had to benefit each other. Each week they used a "merry-go-round" process where each woman would put into a pot say 50 shillings or about 62 cents in USD. They would give that to a different woman each week and she could use the 800 shillings for *anything* she needed other than brewing. Each member would also put into a different pot as much as they could. That pot usually totaled around 3,000 to 5,000 shillings which would also be given to a different woman each week in a similar merry-go-round fashion.

However, with the larger fund there were "strings" and stipulations. Before a woman could receive the money, she had to show the group her business plan and what she would use the money for within that plan. If the group felt the plan was good, the money was given as a gift with no need to pay it back and no rate of interest tacked on. When the next woman was due the funds, she too would have to show the group her business plan for starting her small business and what she would use the money for. But the group also went back to the previous woman to verify she had indeed used the money in the manner stated for her new business. If she did, all was fine. If she did not she was told that she was still loved by all but simply would not be able to continue within the group. Clearly being accountable and taking responsibility were important parts of the group's value system from the very beginning.

Over the next year, two of the 16 decided to go back into brewing and thus were removed from the group.

Yet in that same time period, the remaining 14 had done it! Each had their small business and was making enough money to stay out of brewing, provide food for their family and with luck having some money for school fees when their children were older. They were not living the high life mind you, but they were getting by, even if at times barely.

Then again that's where the group continued to help each other. If one of them was in particular trouble or need they would each chip in what they could to help. It was more than just a group doing business. It was a group of individuals coming together to help each other succeed in a world full of trials and challenges. In that respect they truly had a "heart of peace" and yet they could also be harsh when needed.

As an example, if any of the women were found to be brewing again there would be a warning for them to stop or face being removed from the group. Sadly, in a couple of cases that needed to be done and the number within the group dropped to 12, and then to 11 as one other decided she was good on her own now and did not need the group any more. She has done well for herself, remains good friends with all and has stayed out of brewing, still living on the business she created with the help from the group.

In short, what these women had done was deemed to be impossible by many. In a region where unemployment was off the charts where men and youths stood around with nothing to do as there were simply no jobs, these women created 12 jobs out of thin air! Where no one had created jobs for so long, these women with so little had done it by simply leveraging what they had to create a better life for themselves and their families. To me this was and is simply amazing!

This brings me to how I found Ruth. It is the story of two different people growing up within different cultures located nearly half a world apart yet both making decisions that would eventually lead to their eventual meeting. That in itself seems magical.

I mean think about it. My marriage to your mother needed to end, my relationship with my "significant other" needed to end, I needed to be asked to resign or be fired from the Chamber, I needed my short business relationship with my friends at Hand-to-Hand Global Leadership to create the leadership concept for Jamaica's youth which led me to both Roberta in Jamaica and later Mary Okioma and her NGO in Kenya. I needed to take a leap of faith to come to Kenya against all accepted logic, and I needed to decide to sell everything to go "all in" to create my dream which apparently needed to start in Kenya.

WOW! That's a lot of things to happen for my being in a position to meet Ruth! And yet any other decision in any of the areas above would have created a different time stream and my never having the opportunity to meet or know Ruth. So you might understand more when I say there are no accidents in life… only choices creating an infinite number of possibilities.

Here's how it went down. There was a young man named Andrew who himself had done and experienced things in the post-election violence he was not particularly proud of. To his credit, instead of simply hiding, blaming others, justifying or simply ignoring what had happened, he decided to do something to make up for those terrible things done.

To hear Andrew tell the story it is clear that the cheap illegal alcohol being so easily available was one of the main culprits in the changing of friends who worked and lived together into enemies doing violence upon one another. It was the alcohol that was provided by the many brewers in the area, including Ruth and the women's group mentioned above, that in Andrew's words "gave us the courage to act."

So in the aftermath of the violence, Andrew began forming groups to help find ways of bringing back those who had been forcefully removed from their homes. To do so, the groups he helped form began to create jobs and income to help the economy of the area, provide opportunities for people to work together again and to make amends and to move forward.

In time he heard of a group of brewers who wished to get out of brewing, create "legit" jobs and make a positive contribution to society. He decided to help and began to meet and advise them. He supported the older women who had decided to stop brewing while encouraging others to change their group to be one of non-brewers. He promised them he would help them to the extent he could.

Andrew had done a couple of things with Initiatives of Change in his area and had decided to go to a meeting in Nairobi where I too was attending. In short, he heard me speak about empowerment and self-leadership and decided then and there he wanted me to come to his area to speak to the groups he had helped form.

A couple of months had passed when I got the call from him inviting me to come speak to some 10 groups and spend a week or so in his area. I said I could give him a couple of days so we began to set the days as he chose which of the 10 groups I would speak to. There ended up being four. One was a group of farmers attempting to grow passion fruit, another was a group of families working together to drain a swamp where they would eventually create enough produce to support over 50 families, the third group were youth entrepreneurs with the final group being the former women brewers.

The stage was set until I nearly chose to undo what was about to happen.

It was a few weeks before the upcoming trainings and I was emotionally tired and losing too much weight. It was then a good friend from North Carolina I had met in a leadership conference in New York decided I needed a "mental health" break. I was given the opportunity to meet some people in Italy and to spend some time on the coast with all expenses paid. It was a very generous offer but the trip was going to fall when I was supposed to speak to Andrew's groups.

It was a dilemma and it turned into the classic good angel on one shoulder whispering into one ear why I should keep my word to the groups with the more devilish entity on the other shoulder whispering the opposite advice and why a trip to Italy would be good in the long run for everyone. Deep down I knew I had made a commitment and it was one of the main reasons why I came to Kenya in the first place. At the same time I also felt so tired and exhausted that spending time relaxing with friends in Italy sounded like a little bit of heaven simply a plane reservation away. It was a classic internal battle.

I decided to go to Italy and cancel my obligation to Andrew's groups along with a ton of justifications as to why it was the right thing to do.

Call it God, Allah, Yahweh or the universe stepping in, call it luck... call it what you wish, but I was blocked in my attempts to make the reservation that evening go through on my credit card. The card was fine but the airline here in Kenya was not set up to take reservations via credit card online at that time. In the end I needed to go to their offices at the airport to make the reservation final. So I was to wait till morning.

All night long the debate continued between my spirit and mind with the two characters on my shoulders working as if their souls depended upon their convincing me of what I should do. In the morning I knew. I was going to follow my original commitment to myself and Andrew's groups. So instead of the Italian coast I went to rural Kenya.

The first three sessions with Andrew's groups were all good and I learned a lot as this was my first real trip into rural Kenya on my own. We mostly met outdoors under the shade of a tree or in small rooms with no lighting but all sessions were packed with people with an intense desire to do something to change their lives. In one way it was a powerful reminder to me of what the human spirit could do even in terrible circumstances. Yet in another way it was sad as I sensed very quickly from our discussions that many deep down, especially the youth, did not hold out much hope for their success even as they kept trying.

For anyone to continue to try with a mindset and spirit saying that it would all probably fail in the end is a horrible way to live each day. And yet, here they were still going to try again against all odds not knowing that their own thoughts and doubts were actually going to increase their chances of once again failing.

I did the best I could in those few hours with each group to show them the power of their thoughts and how mindsets are in the end everything as to the realities we create.

It was late afternoon when we started for the last group, the women's group. I will admit I almost said I was too tired and perhaps we could do this group another time. What I was really feeling was a sense of inadequacy in working with a group of former brewers. What could I possibly tell a group of brewers who had been abused by men and left on their own with many children to care for? Did I really have anything that could be of value to these women... after all this is now the real world and not just some mental exercise of what one might do some day. This was as real as it gets and I was a bit scared... perhaps more doubtful of what I was really going to be able to do for them, my experiences with the women of Kibera notwithstanding.

When I arrived the meeting was set up to be in the shade of a big tree in the yard of one of the group members. They had removed a wooden couch and a small wooden coffee table from the home and placed it under the tree so I would be in the shade. They had put small cushions upon the couch and decorated it with the best cloth they had available.

When the meeting started, the women, some of their family members and children sat around on blankets on the ground mostly in the sun. I remember feeling uncomfortable being treated as someone really important yet I also knew they were giving me what they could and I needed to receive that being given with equal respect and dignity. I began to understand the concepts of giving and receiving are two sides of the same coin. One can never give anything and have the good feelings associated with giving without someone else choosing to receive it. By learning to receive I can also help give that same wonderful feeling to someone else wishing to give.

I remember Andrew starting off the session emphasizing I was not a donor but instead a teacher who was going to spend some time with them teaching leadership. I remember starting and at one point the interpreter being changed right in the middle of things. Apparently the interpreter had not eaten much, was running out of energy and beginning to confuse his words. Fortunately Andrew knew English, Kalenjin and Swahili and stepped in to make sure the women understood correctly what I was saying to them!

At the end, the chosen leader of the group for the event stepped up to thank me on behalf of the group, stating the group understood I was not a donor. Still they wished to give me a copy of their proposal of their dream someday. They dreamed of having a dairy herd large enough to take all of their families out of poverty forever. The woman doing the speaking was chosen to lead that day as she was the only one who could understand and speak English well enough to the Mzungu visitor. And though she had only gone to school until the 10th grade (Form 2 in Kenya) her English was amazingly good. And compared to my knowledge of either Kalenjin or Swahili and me with my highfalutin' Master's Degree, it was downright incredible!

The leader's name I came to know later was Ruth.

Of course I accepted their proposal, stating I would read it and would someday return to talk with them again if they would like. I also remember a huge sense within my spirit that I really wanted to help them create their dream of having their dairy herd. Even though it was not what I came to do in Kenya it was something my spirit just wanted to be part of somehow.

I told them I could not fund them but would put out their story on the internet and see what might happen. I also said I would return to see how they were doing. They all clapped but no one believed I would ever return.

As I learned later, the reason no one believed I would return was that everyone who said such things never came back. I also learned I was the first Mzungu to actually come just to speak to them as a women's group. All the other "important visitors" had come via a politician, NGO or organization and the women were simply asked to come wearing their ceremonial dress to dance and sing for the visitor. They would then be given some money for their transportation and that would be it.

So it was a BIG DEAL when I came to speak to the women without all of the pomp most came to the rural areas with: a caravan of cars, support staff and local leaders and Elders falling over themselves trying to impress the visitor. My visit was unusual as it was just me with Andrew, one car and my willingness to spend all of my time just with the group rather than having all of the Elders and politicians give speeches drawing attention to themselves and taking partial credit for my being there.

Looking back, I didn't see how big a deal my being there was yet it was something that had never happened there before – someone coming just to teach women, and former brewers at that, who was not trying to convert them to some religion or another but just wishing to help them become better. Imagine!

Ruth then gave me the ceremonial Calabash with the Kalenjin sour milk which traditionally has the taste of charcoal. And as the women were dancing and singing I took the Calabash and tipped it up expecting the milk to come. Nothing came so I tipped it further upon which it came at such a pace it dribbled out of both sides of my mouth on to the collar of my shirt! Later I saw a picture showing the spilt milk but also a black smudge on my pointed Stevens genetic nose as it had touched the charcoal coating *inside* the Calabash!

Through it all, Ruth was there to help while politely dabbing the milk from my shirt and smudges from my nose. Then she took my hand to lead me to the house where food would be served. No individual or member of royalty has ever been treated with more respect and grace than I was that day.

As we were about to leave, Ruth again took my arm to lead me to the group and the parade process we would follow to where the car was parked. I do not know why, guys, and it might embarrass you a bit hearing this from your dad, but I needed, no I wanted to hold her hand. But Ruth's grip was so firm on my arm that I could only grasp one of her fingers as we walked to the awaiting car with Ruth and the group singing.

There was something about Ruth's presence, a deeper wisdom within her eyes, a beauty and strength from within I could sense and I found myself wishing I could stay and talk with her, to find out more about who she was and about her life. But it was time to go.

I remember sitting in the back seat of the vehicle and as we drove away I turned to find her from among the crowd waving us goodbye. I found her and our eyes met. It wasn't as I recall "*love*" per se. It was more of an "I see you and I acknowledge and respect who you are" type of look. Ruth told me later the other women saw me looking for her and all began to laugh and shout, "Ruth is going to America! Ruth is going to go to America!"

On the way home I asked Andrew who she was and he told me what he knew. I mentioned I wanted to meet her again to get to know more about her. He seemed genuinely pleased and a bit "tickled" that this old Mzungu seemed to be smitten with a Kalenjin woman but said he would find out more and whether another visit would be appropriate.

About a week after returning to Nairobi, I received an email from Andrew with his report from his investigation of Ruth. It was a report which the American CIA would have been in awe of I think. He seemed to know everything including how many times she had been to the hospital and what people thought it was about! The bottom line and most important to me was she was single although I would learn later that in Kenya the fact that one was single could be a bit more complicated than in America. Andrew told me he had spoken with Ruth and she indicated it would be OK for me to call her if I wished.

Ruth confessed to me later she was a bit confused as to why I wished to call her, but chalked it up to her being the best member of the group in her English and that I might be serious about returning to work with them. So Ruth sent me an SMS with her name and phone number the next day as Andrew had suggested.

A few weeks later I did return and stayed with Ruth in her home which created quite a ruckus I later found out. On Andrew's part, he knew Ruth was single but he also knew she had been married once before in a "cultural" Kalenjin wedding which would be a marriage recognized in Kenya but nowhere else. And as I was to find out, the polygamy laws in Kenya can make marriages and families pretty confusing to an American not used to such things.

Andrew also knew (saying nothing to me) that Ruth had also been culturally divorced, meaning that both families had gotten together and agreed that the couple should not be married anymore. Apparently this does not happen often in Kenya and usually implies something extremely serious had happened... so serious that both families agreed that Ruth and her husband should no longer be married.

Later I would learn that Ruth's husband had taken a second wife with the second wife not wishing to always be the second wife. So she tried to kill Ruth with poison disguised as medicine when Ruth was pregnant and feeling ill. After taking it, Ruth became extremely sick, the baby was lost and Ruth nearly died. If it had not been for a friend realizing what was happening, Ruth would have died. But her friend got her away from there and over time and with medical treatment she recovered. Later the families agreed to the divorce. It was after that experience Ruth, now on her own, attempted various jobs for income and later turned to brewing in order to survive.

Anyway, Andrew *thought* everything would be OK but in Kenya one never knows if a former family member might feel Ruth should never be with anyone else again and come with friends to do harm to either Ruth, the other man or both. So he and a friend took turns the evenings I was visiting guarding the house discreetly out of sight.

I now understand it is not that uncommon for a group of uncles, cousins or friends of a particular family who do not believe a woman who had been part of their family should be seeing anyone to decide to break into the woman's home in order to beat the man and the woman terribly. This could happen to a woman even if her husband had died and she finally decided to be with someone else.

Like I said before, don't try to put this into context from what you have experienced or learned in your life for it simply will not nor could it make any sense. Anyway, unknown to me, for the two nights I was there, Andrew and friends guarded the house just out of sight to make sure nothing happened.

Of course, I was totally unaware of any of this including the previous marriage and the poisoning. I was just a guy happily and obviously blindly getting to know a woman who seemed to be someone special.

And of course the more I learned, the more I knew it was true. Ruth was and is incredible in so many ways.

The other part of the ruckus from my staying with Ruth was from the Elders. It seems they were angry at both Andrew and Ruth for my staying in Ruth's home. Not because I was a man and she was a woman but because I was a Mzungu and I must stay in one of the "nicer" homes in the area, be given better sleeping quarters, better food etc. They could not believe a Mzungu would willingly want to stay in Ruth's home where there was no electricity, no plumbing and only a community outdoor toilet.

It was only after I told Andrew to tell the Elders it was my choice to stay with Ruth and that I was just fine did they leave feeling satisfied I was being treated respectfully. It was the beginning of their mindsets and mine about each other being ripped apart and becoming forever changed. Direct contact and talking to each other has a way of doing that in the world. Who knew?

As long as it was my choice and I wasn't being forced, the Elders calmed down. It was a turning point for many I think. They began to see I didn't feel superior and was just fine living just as they did while eating the same foods they ate every day: mostly ugali and vegetables along with chapattis if there was enough money. Meat *might* be eaten but ONLY on a very special occasion as it was just too expensive for most to buy. In most cases the meat would be goat, which really doesn't taste all that baaaaad! Sorry... couldn't resist!

I began to visit whenever I could which meant about once every three weeks or so. Each visit was unique. I began to speak with many groups who heard the Mzungu was at Ruth's and hoped I would speak to them about leadership. Many truly wanted to learn what I had to offer. Many only wanted me to hear and see what they were attempting to do so that I might fund them. In Kenya, there is no shyness of asking people for money especially if the person is a Mzungu, whom everyone knows has to be rich.

I also began to feel like the "Godfather." I literally had people lining up to ask for money or a favor which would always lead to money: a sick child, school fees for their children who without education will be poor forever, orphans, medicine, funds for a school facility or an entrepreneur wanting startup capital. Almost all were gracious and understanding when I said no although there were a few who became angry.

I think from their viewpoint, since their mindset "knew" I had money the only reason I was saying no was that I simply did not wish to help THEM. One in particular I will simply refer to as the "Red Hat" due to him always wearing that particular color of hat.

He tried to get others to do harm to both Ruth and me and did his best to destroy the women's group which

I would end up choosing to help. Usually he shot his mouth off when he was drunk but I cannot deny that it became a concern a few times. I was glad to know both the Area Police Chief and some of the Elders were paying close attention to Ruth's home in case something might happen late some evening when I was not there.

Fortunately few listened to him as they believed I was there to help and not to do the self-serving things the Red Hat was suggesting. In time he gave up and is harassing other people now. I should probably add that a lot of people including me wear red hats at times so people should not look suspiciously at everyone wearing a red hat when they come to visit us in Center Kwanza!

In a way it occurred to me this is what many people who settled in the Wild West of our country's history may have endured. There may have been law enforcement, but they were far away and it would take time to get word to them and more time for help to come. In the meantime, if a rowdy group of drunkards decided to leave the saloon to teach someone a lesson, it would be up to those in the area to protect themselves and perhaps their neighbors if necessary.

It truly was and is like that with us at times. Although few have guns in rural Kenya (mostly knives, axes, bows and arrows and pangas) anything can happen and does! Sadly, more guns are finding their way into the country. I have concluded that people without guns kill people just as they do with guns. So to me the only real question in the debate of guns or no guns is simply how easy does a society wish to make it to kill another, how fast and from what distance? Just saying...

Yet for me, being given opportunities to help so many yet having to say no was incredibly stressful. My ability to be of real help to others with very legitimate and in so many cases desperate needs was limited as, truthfully, I was barely able to pay my own bills let alone provide what was needed to build the leadership program.

I have never taken emotional stress well. These were mothers, fathers, grandparents or young people all humbly asking, many with sincere tears in their eyes, as they spoke of the needs of their loved ones or of their own need to survive in a way that gave their life meaning. It was so hard to say no. In time word spread that the Mzungu either had a cold heart or he was sincere in his not being able to help and in time the requests began to slow down.

However, even with no money myself, I couldn't say no to everyone and I helped those I could. Somehow I would find a way. Yet deciding who to help and who I would not was almost as difficult as saying no. In some cases my helping or not would be a life changer, and knowing that also added to my thinking and understanding of what kind of help would be beneficial in the long run and what kind would simply be squandered and wasted.

The Starfish story came in handy here… you know, the one where a young man was walking along the beach when he came upon hundreds of stranded starfish all dead or dying. He was able to reach one and carefully put it back into the deeper waters of the ocean. People watching then asked why he helped the one as saving one starfish would not make any difference in the scheme of things. The young man responded, "It made a difference to that one starfish."

I also began to make a list of people I would like to help if I could somehow find the resources to give – always as a gift that did not need to be paid back but having follow-ups to keep everyone accountable. People needed to know if the Mzungu gave money there would be strict accountability, and if those receiving did not work hard or use the money in the intended way, the money would dry up immediately. What I would find out later through experience is that some simply didn't care if the money dried up. They wanted money now and for them money now even if stopped was better than no money at all.

Ruth would later share with me the details of each person and more of their personal story. It seems everyone knew and respected Ruth. She was a "truthsayer" and actually did what she stated she would do. She was honest and above all, if asked to help even if she had nothing, she would find something to give as that was part of who she was. It was not uncommon, for example, for Ruth to go to a fundraising gathering or "Harambee" having no money to give but perhaps bringing two ears of maize and offering them up for auction with the proceeds becoming her contribution to the fundraising.

Some people speak of doing good things and talk about giving being more important than receiving but I tell you Ruth is in fact a person who does it all and willingly gives with no thought of getting anything in return. Like I said, I was learning just how special she really was. Even today I will sometimes find myself back in my traditional mindsets and begin to rant about not being able to help everyone as we too have so little and why should we have to when no one else within their family who could are doing anything to help... yadda, yadda, yadda. Most times Ruth just looks at me, smiles and says, "Because they need help and they asked." Game over.

I am reminded of the verses in the Christian Bible which asks if the people needed clothes, or food or water or shelter did I help or did I keep what I had for myself? (James 2: 14-18) I have learned much from Ruth in regard to giving with a true heart and admit to having to work hard to undo many of the mindsets I had created from my capitalistic background.

By the way, I think the mistake too many people and organizations make when they attempt to help others in developing countries is trying to put the things to be done into their own existing mindsets. They still see the world of those they are attempting to help through the eyes of their own lives and experiences and, quite honestly, there will be few mental matches that will create a true understanding. They will see, they will interpret but it will in the end be only their illusion. So much harm has been done with people having the best of intentions.

A small example is the used clothing given by so many church organizations and aid programs to the people of Kenya and Africa. To be honest, it has been effective if the goal was only to make sure the people, especially the children of Kenya, had adequate clothes to wear. Yet if the goal was to help the people of Kenya build a clothing industry where they would in time clothe themselves, then the aid has been a disaster.

In the past, the government of Kenya has tried to pass laws to increase taxes on incoming clothing in order to protect their own budding clothing industry only to have the people clearly voice their opposition. In short, the people of Kenya are now dependent upon those same organizations for their clothing now and into the future. That creation of dependency is one of the most hurtful and harmful things aid organizations have done to Kenyans and Africa as a whole I believe. Good intentions perhaps but destructive in the long run.

I often tell any group who might listen that if they must give clothing then also follow it up with sewing machines, cloth and training for youth and women so they can make clothes for themselves and others as a small business. Plus, those helping to develop these new entrepreneurs should also set up markets within their own country or region for the purchasing of the clothing or products made by those new entrepreneurs. In that way the budding businesses would be able to compete with the cheap clothing industry within Kenya. The combination of that would make a real difference in both the short and long term, assuming the selection of those being helped was tied to careful screenings and accountability. But flooding the market with cheap clothing needs to stop if people truly care about those they are wishing to help. But I am wandering from my story...

The more Ruth explained about people and why things happened the way they did, the more I began to understand the Kalenjin culture and Kenya better. I began to realize I simply had nothing in my learning or experience for my mind to match in order to interpret correctly what I was now seeing and experiencing. In so many ways what on the surface seemed understandable was becoming a totally new world.

I remember one day Ruth and I had gone to her mother's home which is about a four-hour walk from where we were in Center Kwanza. We took boda bodas (motorbikes) to save time. On the way back it was night and a full moon shone over the African landscape. It had rained so the roads had become too muddy for transport so we decided to walk the rest of the way. It was truly magical, guys.

The moon was so bright even I could see in the dark as we walked down from the large hills near Center Kwanza. In the distance we could hear the chants and choruses of men and boys singing the traditional African songs as various male circumcision ceremonies were being performed. I truly knew then that I was not in Kansas anymore. Ruth would tell me the stories of Kalenjin culture and of all of the places and people we passed by on our way home. Kenya was becoming more part of my life than I ever imagined it would.

I continued to visit and stay with Ruth over the next year. Then one day as I was traveling to see her I knew I wanted to ask her to marry me. What I didn't know is whether her Kalenjin culture would make it possible for her to say yes or even if she would.

We had shared so much and there was some fear on my part of messing up a great friendship by proposing marriage. I also had no clue as to how this marriage would work. My work would be mostly in Nairobi, her work with young people and groups and of course the dairy group to be was in Center Kwanza. She was taking care of two children in what we would call a foster care kind of arrangement but in reality was much different in Kalenjin culture. Young Judith was nine years old and Ron, who was 17 and out on his own. How would that work? They were her children to care for and yet they were not.

Perhaps I should take a moment and attempt to explain that last statement.

One of the outcomes of Ruth's poisoning was her not being able to have children. And since Ruth was above 40 years of age, in her culture she was too old for any Kalenjin man of credibility and integrity to marry. Someone may want her for a second or third wife but Ruth was not so disposed to be that.

So prior to meeting me, she was certain she would grow old and have no children of her own who would take care of her. So when two women at different times ran into hardships and were unable to take care of their children, the community and family came together to see how they could help raise the children. It was only natural for Ruth to volunteer to raise two over time – Judith and Ron.

But remember what I said above about learning something and trying to make sense of it by matching it with what we have learned about families and what they should or should not be like. If we match it to what we know, what we will interpret and understand will make sense to us but it will be only illusion and not close to what is truly there. Such has been my challenges with trying to get a handle of the concept of family structures in Kenyan society.

In many ways their family structures are better and closer than ours and in other ways they seem to be more dysfunctional. I have learned that in both cultures, Kalenjin and Nebraskan, to grasp them one needs to put all judgment aside and simply learn. They both work and yet both are sometimes broken too. They just are what they have developed to be with the overall intention of doing the right thing.

So how would all of this work for Ruth and me? Would she move to Nairobi? What would then happen to the children she was caring for or the groups that Ruth was so much the heart of? Would we go to the U.S. eventually if my work permits failed to materialize and if so would we bring the children when they are not officially hers by any standard that the United States Department of Immigration would recognize? How would the two of you react? How would my mother and sisters react and would doing this take me away from my dream or help create it?

All of these questions were rattling around my mind as I took the seven-hour shuttle ride from Nairobi to Eldoret and then Center Kwanza along what I later learned was the world's fourth most dangerous roadway! I just remember feeling very unsettled yet having a deep knowing I wished Ruth to be in my life for the days that still remained for me in this world.

I also remember sending Ruth some texts (SMS) via phone and at one point sent one asking what she thought about our relationship. When she responded favorably (meaning she didn't say it sucked) I sent another one saying since that was the case I would have a personal question I would ask her later that night after everyone had gone to bed.

Again, you may not wish to hear this from your dad but my heart was literally pounding, and when a lot of time passed with no response from Ruth I began to make up all sorts of things, mostly that she was going to say no. My emotions were no different from the first time I asked Billye Jo May if she wanted to "go steady" in the 9th grade!

As it was, Ruth did not understand the American concept of the question I was going to ask to be a marriage proposal. To her she just knew I was going to ask a question.

Anyway, that evening I decided to actually ask her. At first I thought her response was going to be no as she stated that in her culture there was only one reason to become married and that was to have children. And since she could no longer have children, marriage was not thinkable. To my American mind that was a no. Bummer.

I think I said something about already having two amazing and challenging sons and at my age had no need to do all of that again... or something like that. I think I also stated I wanted to live my life with her and to have her in my life for however long God blessed us to be together and not having more children was just fine with me.

She said she had just assumed I would want to have children otherwise why marry? So she wanted me to understand that she could not so I would not be deceived and so I could understand why marriage was not possible. She then stated that if I still wanted to marry her knowing that children were out of the question then she would agree to that. WHEW!

That was one of the three happiest moments of my life (the other two being the two of you being born into my world). I can say nearly three years later, each day Ruth has been in my life has continued to be happy and amazing even with all the twists and turns life has thrown our way... and there have certainly been plenty of those!

Of course when we told everyone our intentions there were very mixed reactions with the most surprising being from our mothers – both Ruth's and mine. Ruth's father had died long before but the first thought of her mother and family was why would a Mzungu like me want to marry someone as old as

Ruth?! Now counter that with Nebraskan culture with people asking the exact opposite question, "Why would a woman so much younger want to marry an old guy like me?"

Your Grandmother DJ's reaction and that of your Aunt Danna, my youngest sister, was cautiously neutral... meaning that they did not support, nor did they oppose until they ascertained whether or not I was out of my mind. I remember my mother asking, "How do you think you can take on more responsibilities when you are barely able to keep yourself above water?" Score one for DJ.

Of course it was a fair question and perhaps one of the biggest differences your Grandmother DJ and I have always had. She grew up during the Great Depression where saving, financial stability and careful planning were paramount to success and life. And though I do not disagree with those principles, I do not think they should be the controlling factors in one's actions either. There are times for a leap of faith in order to go down that road less traveled. So my mother's reaction was predictable and yet I will admit to being disappointed there was no cheering, congratulations or wanting to know all about their new daughter-in-law or sister-in-law to be.

Having said that, in time they were convinced that my decision was indeed best for me and they have been nothing but totally supportive in every way to both

Ruth and me. They were concerned first with my well-being and stability and from that perspective were both very loving and caring for their son and "big bro."

The two of you plus your Aunt Cris and her husband Ron were immediately supportive and that truly meant a lot… more than you may ever know at this point in your lives.

I should also say that your mother and Rob were also very supportive and happy at the news and that too was nice and helpful, especially since Ruth would carry your mother's maiden name once she became Ruth Jepngetich Bernard-Stevens! ☺ And here your mom thought if she married and took the name of her spouse that the Bernard name would no longer continue which was the reason your mom and I hyphenated our last names in the first place! Life has a lot of interesting twists and turns, doesn't it?!

I remember inviting all of the immediate family knowing full well the trip would be too much for anyone to manage. So you can imagine I was super excited when I heard you, David, and your wife Sarah would be coming!

Anyway, that is how I met Ruth and how we decided to marry.

Let me add mostly for your sake, Matt, there were actually two weddings. The official one for Kenya was the Engagement Ceremony and for that we did a somewhat modified yet traditional Kalenjin ceremony which comprised negotiating for cows.

At first I had the point of view that negotiating for cows to pay my future wife's family for the right to marry their daughter was silly. I mean really, comparing the value of Ruth to cows! Really?

Yet being here and learning of the huge value dairy cows and goats have been throughout history to the lives of the millions of poor in Africa, and in this case Kenya, it is indeed very symbolic of the value one places upon the other. I think it's not much different from the notion we have that the size of the diamond and the ring is an indication of how much we value our future wife. We value a woman to a "rock" (diamond) that is not scarce and can be found in almost any small town anywhere in the world? Really?

I remember us walking to the home of Ruth's mother when I was able to say the only thing I was allowed to say during the whole Engagement Ceremony. As we approached the door, Ruth's family came out and welcomed us while asking the nature of our visit which of course they all knew very well. To wit I said on behalf of myself and my "family," "We have lost our most valued calf and we believe the calf may have wandered here. Have you found her?" Note the "we" as it is indicative of the whole family and not just me.

They responded they may have found such a calf and we should all come in to see for sure. Then they asked the girls in the other room to come out and if the calf was there for me to identify it. When I saw Ruth, I took a "flower" necklace and placed it over her head and around her neck. She was then asked to identify the person in the room she was willing to leave with, upon which she placed a "flower" necklace over my head and around my neck. I put the word "flower" in quotation marks as they were not really flowers at all, just shiny tinsel-like decorations that they called flowers. Anyway, it was then everyone sat down to get to the negotiations which quickly became very serious and intense!

My negotiating "team" had met the night before to plan our strategy. My surrogate mother and father would be Andrew's parents, David and Rachel. They would be crucial as the entire negotiations would be in Kalenjin so I would have no clue what was being said nor would I be permitted to say anything once the negotiations began! I had to trust my family to do the best for me. In this sense it truly is one family asking another for the permission to take one of their daughters to care for forever more.

The planning session got serious when they realized how little money I had and how few cows I could actually buy. After I told them I might be able to buy a liver, heart, two legs and a head of one cow but that was about it, I could see the concern in their eyes and someone quietly stated, "Wow, I've never negotiated from nothing before. How will we do that?"

Fortunately my years of legislative conniving and plotting came to our rescue and I threw out a plan of attack they eventually agreed to after a few cultural modifications. We would take the differences in American and Kalenjin cultures and create a positive!

In short, the next day my acting father and mother argued two basic points: one, that according to American custom it was the bride's family who pays for all of the wedding expenses, in this case the buying of the cows; and two, whether they agree or not to terms in the end it will not matter for if there is no agreement, Ruth and David being old will simply go to Nairobi and be married there under church and American tradition and the family would get nothing.

Ruth's negotiating team's opening salvo came from the Old Testament. I remember thinking Oh God NOT the Old Testament! Nothing but plagues, demons, pestilence and souls being damned to hell if they didn't do something to please Yahweh ever comes from the Old Testament! They had found a verse which indicated if I didn't pay up big, God would not be pleased. Touché! Point and counter-point!

So we started from the number zero but my team argued since David (me) wanted to honor Kalenjin tradition he was willing to negotiate even though his culture did not demand it. He was willing to "compromise" his traditions to bring our two cultures together. They of course started from a much higher number and since we were in their home under Kalenjin tradition, they stayed with a strict Kalenjin mindset.

I was later told by Andrew there was an attempt to compromise "halfway" but that number was below anything Ruth's family had EVER negotiated before and their position seemed to harden by the minute. What was not being said was that all of their neighbors would no doubt ridicule them if they agreed to a lower number especially since the negotiations were with someone most perceived as being a rich Mzungu. They would look like terribly weak negotiators or else Ruth was not very valuable due to her age!

I could sense and see that some in Ruth's family were not happy and my team was showing some tension as well, yet at the same time I had no idea what was being said or why. I remember feeling somewhat panicky, looking toward Ruth who was not looking at me. But her best friend Nancy looked back, smiled and gave a secret thumbs up which made me feel a bit better. A thought did briefly cross my mind that I could be walking toward the gallows and she would still give me that same thumbs up with a smile that all would be OK.

In the end, two people stood and sealed the deal. One was Rachel, my surrogate mother. She firmly reminded them I did not have to negotiate at all from my culture's perspective, so they could either agree to the number that was "halfway" or not. If they did not, Ruth and David would go and be married anyway in the American tradition. It was their call.

I was really glad she was on my side! Yet from my political experience I could sense the Elder men on Ruth's team did not wish to be pushed into a decision by a woman and my political instincts were bracing for the "push back" I knew was about to come.

It was then the second person, who was the eldest of the Elders from Ruth's family having three wives of his own, rose to speak. He had listened quietly saying nothing but then stood, and after speaking all further discussion ceased. He simply stated, "We all know David does not have to follow our customs yet he has decided to honor us by doing so. We have a choice. We can say no and stand for our pride and a number we think he should pay and drive both him and Ruth away or we can decide here and now we will do what needs to be done to bring the cultures of America and Kalenjin together as one in this family." Game over.

Matt, since David was here, he was technically the senior member of our family present and as such it was his responsibility to agree or not agree on my behalf. Of course no one bothered to tell him that minor detail prior to the moment the senior Elders of Ruth's family asked him if the agreement reached was acceptable!

I shall always remember the startled look on his face at being suddenly asked so direct a question with everyone staring at him waiting for his answer as he listened to the translation! I recall David looking at me with a "deer in the headlights" look, not wanting to make a mistake at this level with my life hanging in the balance of what was clearly going to be his decision!

I told him, "It's your call and don't let the fact that my life-long happiness is in your hands worry you at all at this moment!" Yet I tried to use a tone of voice indicating that all was well even though I still had no idea what agreement had been reached. I had faith that if my "surrogate family" felt it was good I would be OK with it as well. David's legislative skills of deciding how to vote came to his aid once more as he agreed to the terms on behalf of our family and the agreement was accepted.

At that, all opposition melted away with the agreed upon number of cows and a sheep thrown in for Ruth's mother, written down on paper. The representatives from both families along with Ruth and I signed the handwritten settlement and the celebration began which was a wonderful lunch of rice, red beans, meat, chapattis and of course sour milk.

It was at that moment Ruth and I were officially married in Kenya... no church, no certificates, just two families coming together and agreeing their "children" can marry. Of course these children were awfully old and such a cultural marriage would not be recognized by most of the world. So Ruth and I also did the official Justice of the Peace type marriage in Nairobi about a week or so after David and Sarah left just to make sure all of the legal bases were covered.

Such as it was and such was the time my roots in Kenya grew a bit deeper.

Love,
Dad

This is Mary, one of the four elder women who began the I'nget Nge'tiet Women's Group.

May 15, 2014

My first self-leadership and empowerment training with the I'nget Nge'tiet Women's Group.

Ruth presenting me with the honor of a ceremonial Calabash full of traditional sour milk as the training concluded.

191

David, his wife Sarah and I just prior to leaving for the engagement ceremony in Ruth's family home.

Ruth's negotiating team who set the stage by first quoting from the Old Testament!

My negotiating team during a rather "tense" moment.

Ruth signing the officially agreed upon engagement agreement. And with that, we were officially married within the Kalenjin culture!

Ruth and I after the more internationally accepted wedding in Nairobi.

June 23, 2014

Dear David and Matt

I woke up in a reflective mood this morning so am wanting to say some things you may or may not understand, not because of any inability on your part but perhaps my poor attempts to find the right words to convey my thoughts adequately. And yet, it is part of what I believe to be true and has much bearing on what I try to transfer to my life and to those in my trainings. And whether you agree or not with the ideas I am about to share with you, they will at least give an insight to what drives me and some of the concepts I teach in order to help people become more than what they were just a moment before.

Let me start with two questions needing to be asked, understood and accepted if we wish to ever lead ourselves to becoming who we were created to be: "What am I willing to put myself in harm's way for?" and "What am I supposed to do?"

The only way I know to find those answers is to shut down the mind for a moment and go within one's self asking some extremely tough questions while at the same time giving blunt, honest, and sincere answers *without judgment*. This in itself is not easy as most of us will lie to ourselves not wishing to face the truth concerning the questions being asked. Yet if we work at it over time it will become easier and the answers clearer. For when we go within ourselves we are traveling the path toward our own spirit which has power and wisdom beyond our present understandings.

Let me say one other thing while I am on this point. I have not found anyone anywhere who, when truly connecting with their inner spirit, desired anything that would be deliberately harmful to others. Never! For whenever we touch the depth of our true spirit we are touching the spirit of that which created us. Whether one calls it God, Allah, Yahweh, the Great Spirit, the universe, or the creator of all, it is still that which has been within each of us from the moment of our creation.

That spirit does not hate. That spirit does not judge. That spirit does not deliberately harm another. That spirit is loving, compassionate, and caring in ways powerful enough to change the world if given a chance. It is the spirit hidden that one needs to touch when asking the questions above. When one does, the answers discovered may be radically different from what one might have first imagined.

To find our answers we each have to travel inward. There are many religions in the world and at their cores are many of the same concepts. I would probably identify myself as a "modified" Christian. That fact alone might elicit either joy or fear depending upon the knowledge and mindsets of those reading this. For as the two of you know, Christians have been responsible for much hate, destruction and death in the world as well as some amazingly good things too. So just saying one is a Christian or a Hindu or Muslim or anything else doesn't really say much until one sees their true heart through their actual deeds and behavior. Those will tell anyone observing more about who they are than the words being said. For in my experience, many people who I would classify as evil by their own choices have disguised their actions by cloaking themselves with religious clothing, scripture, dogma or patriotic symbols and flags.

Let me pick some verses from various religious texts which have greatly influenced my thinking. The first comes from the New Testament book of Luke and can be found by going to Chapter 17 verses 20-21 if either of you would care to read it. In this case the quote is coming from the King James Version:

> (20) And when he was demanded by the Pharisees when the kingdom of God should come, he answered them and said, "The kingdom of God cometh not with observation: (21) Neither shall they say, Lo here! Or, lo there! ***for, behold the kingdom of God is within you.***" (emphasis added)

I find this concept in almost all religious texts or writings. And though I am not a deep scholar of religious studies, I have found some examples for you to consider:

- The Buddha apparently said in essence the same thing when he stated, "O man, you don't need to search for God anywhere. You are God yourself."

- In the Biblical Book of John 1:13: "We know that He dwell in us because he has given us of his Spirit."

- In the Bhgavad Gita we find:
  "God dwelleth in all hearts."

- In the Upanishads (Hindu) one finds:
  "The one God hidden in all living things."

- And as stated in the Holy Qur'an:

  We were with Muhammad on a journey, and some men stood up repeating aloud, "God is most great," and the Rasul said, "O men! Be easy on yourselves, and do not distress yourselves by raising your voices, verily you do not call to one deaf or absent, but verily to one who heareth and seeth; and He is with you; and He to whom you pray is nearer to you than the neck of your camel."

I bring this up only to emphasize the deeper meaning behind an individual going inward for answers by asking, "For what am I willing to put myself in harm's way and what am I supposed to do?" It is not a simple matter. In order to find those answers we need to once again become explorers, seekers of truth, curious to know new things while at the same time being brutally honest when answering the tough questions.

We must return to the way we once were – children with insatiable curiosity. It was not that long ago when each of us deliberately struggled to simply roll over as a baby so as to see what was on the "other side." Later, we crawled to explore, then began "cruising" or walking while holding on for dear life as again we went exploring into unknown worlds. Later we walked on our own then ran to see what was "over there." For it is in that frame of mind we will find new answers, new realities, as we once more explore inward to see what is beyond our sight or scope of knowledge. I think that is what Christ was referring to when he said according to Matthew:

> At that time the disciples came to Jesus and asked, "Who is the greatest in the kingdom of Heaven?"
>
> He called a little child and had him stand among them. And he said, "I tell you the truth, unless you change and *become like little children*, you will never enter the kingdom of Heaven. Therefore, whoever humbles himself like this child is the greatest in the kingdom of Heaven." (Matthew 18: 1-4)

Many people do not travel down this inward path of inquiry. Perhaps they are fearful of what they might find or what it will mean for their past decisions, their present actions and their future. And yet for those afraid or not willing to do the work, it might help to know those behaviors are simply reactions to existing mindsets. Yet we can feed and/or create any mindset we wish and as such, our reality of fear doesn't have to be.

It might also help to know our brains have a tendency to be lazy, and while not wanting to work very hard, they still above all love to remain in control. In fact too many of us have let our minds take us wherever it desired and whenever we attempt to take over control as when we attempt not to react but respond, our minds will tell us in so many ways why we should not do that. Our minds can be very convincing while bringing up a myriad of justifications geared to make us feel OK if we and our inner spirit would quit trying to take control of our lives and simply let it (our mind) roll along unfettered thus allowing it to manipulate us like puppets on a string in terms of how we react, feel and behave.

It is a huge challenge to get control of our minds and connect ourselves with our spirit. Yet once accomplished, the combination of spirit and mind together giving all each has to offer to get us where we truly wish to go... well let me just say that the power of that combination is beyond our comprehension. It is from this combined power that dreams can become real. It is from this power and place that the human spirit can indeed transcend all things and become more than even our wildest imaginations could have envisioned.

I believe that is why so many people, groups, families, businesses and projects fail in the end. It is not because their intentions were not good. It is not because the training was bad. It is because they mostly ignore the critical building blocks creating the foundations for sustainability and resilience. The essence for those blocks can only be discovered from deep within the spirit of our humanity. Until that is touched and people learn who they truly are, what they need to be, where they need to go and believe in their inner power to do exactly that, the efforts for the change desired in today's world will be unsustainable and sadly, unfulfilled.

Now let me be clear. Just because I or anyone else does the above does not mean we will get what we want. For as I said before, it is a chaotic universe we exist in where bad things can happen to good people and good things happen to bad people. There are no guarantees except one. IF one thinks and aligns one's thoughts, choices and actions to their inner spirit through core values and purpose, then whatever actions they take along that path will bring joy, purpose, commitment, passion and meaning to each moment of all the days they get to experience *regardless of what happens.* And in the end, who could ask for anything more?

OK... glad I got that out of my system! WHEW!

I think I left off in my last letter with Ruth and I becoming married. Of course with that came changes in both of our lives that are still and will continue to play out as time goes on. I find it interesting that I had just given up thinking I would ever have anyone else in my life and had accepted the fact I was meant to go it alone. I had actually told God I was OK with it if that was to be my fate. It was about two weeks after letting go of the perpetual searching for "the one" when Ruth's spirit touched mine. I find this fascinating and let me say this once again, "Sometimes to get to where one wishes to go one needs to let go first."

I think for the two of you it might be comforting to know that your mother found happiness when she married your stepdad Rob, as many years later I too found happiness with Ruth, your African stepmother now. For me Ruth is the person I had always yearned for but had lost hope of ever finding, as awkward as that may sound to two young men hearing it from their father.

Our being married meant I would be returning to Center Kwanza near Jua Kali more often. As I did, people began to realize Ruth was not going to run away with the Mzungu to America and leave them without another thought. There was my work in Nairobi and Kenya in general and her work with groups in her area that together we would continue being part of as best we could. In time people in Ruth's home area realized

I was now part of their community and would continue to be so as long as I was able to remain in Kenya. The fact that we did not leave I think surprised and pleased almost everyone.

I think I still need to explain to you how all of these projects and various decisions to help people here actually began. It was clearly not my intention to be a "giver" of money to people here in Kenya. That seemed to be too much of a stretch in terms of my financial status and capabilities. And yet that is exactly what happened in spite of my efforts to resist it.

It began obviously with the women's group and their dream to have a dairy herd. I was compelled by their story and meeting them showed me their courage and the difficulties they each had faced throughout their lives. I began to sense the hopelessness that can come from not being able to feed one's children, or if a child or even themselves became ill when there was no money to transport them to a hospital or to pay for any medicines a doctor may prescribe.

The more I got to know and see and the more people began to open up and share with me, I became more aware of the sense of survival that had overtaken so many people along with the attitude "whatever it takes to bring food to the table or to pay for a school fee will be done" with the only ethical question being the survival of one's family. I began to understand the terrible internal struggles that take place within people wishing and wanting to do the right thing yet choosing to compromise those desires in order to survive.

I was beginning to see the people of Kenya with a deeper understanding and I wanted to help, but not just to reinforce their desire to survive, meaning their asking for money and saying whatever was necessary to get money from someone. I wanted to help in a way that continued to feed the good within each of them while at the same time helping each choose to think and act to "be" who they were created to be. If they could do that and learn to believe by taking a step at a time they could indeed create their dream, well then all would be as it should be. But I have to say, knowing what I wanted to do and actually doing it has been an extremely slippery slope to walk.

I sometimes have asked students in rural Kenya to tell me about their families and past history. In nearly all cases their grandparents were poor (not in spirit or in character perhaps), their parents were poor, and they as their children were also poor. And with all of that history and assuming they continued to think and act in the ways they had been taught by their families in the past, what might they predict the future of their children to be?

And though it seemed to be a simple question, it began a discussion that inevitably led to a sense by all that when looking at their past it would in time mirror their own futures and most likely that of their children. It was a sobering reality check for almost everyone. It was as if I could see the hopes and dreams of their imagined futures being dashed as the cold waters of perceived reality washed over them.

It did not take long for most of the students to realize if they continued to think and act in the same ways as those before them, their real future was pretty predictable. Yet from that sense of gloom was also a glimmer of hope with the possibility of that glimmer growing into a brilliant flame having the potential of bringing into their lives a new reality. It would be a reality where dreams could become real with each dreamer having the ability to "change their stars." That glimmer of hope came from a question that always found its way to their consciousness:

> *"What if we learned to think*
> *and do things differently?"*

And there it was, their first sense they may have the power within themselves to create who and what they would be in their future. And with that sense came more questions and a higher sense of curiosity about the potential of new possibilities. The more curious they became, the more information they began to soak in and with each bit of new information gathered, new links within their minds began to form. Those links if fed over time would grow until new links and mindsets would be created about life, their role within it, the infinite possibilities of every moment and the amazing power within everyone to create a future and being of their own choice. They began to realize the true power of the mind when connected to the infinite power of the inner spirit and the potential of creating infinite realities – realities where indeed dreams could come true.

For the first time, many began to sense they may not be trapped by poverty or their lack of schooling, gender or social and cultural beliefs. Perhaps for the first time, many began to doubt the truth of what had previously been created within their own minds of what their life was going to be. Some began to sense that what they "knew" was in fact a prison from which their realities had been created, that it was not in what was known but what was unknown which would set them free.

And from those beginning moments of discussion, nothing was ever the same again.

In Kenya as in much of the world's developing nations, there is a vast and growing number of young people (aged 18 to 35) who are frustrated and whose experiences have led them to believe there is little hope. They have been in what I call "survival mode" for most of their lives and they do not see anything coming that will change that. When they were young children they had hope, yet as they grew in experience, that hope turned to frustration and in some parts of the world that frustration has turned to anger, corruption and violence. David, you have seen it first-hand here and Matt, I know you have experienced similar things in the United States.

When working with the youth of Africa and specifically Kenya and East Africa, I have found them to be some of the brightest and most gifted individuals I have met anywhere in the world. They also know the right things to say when asked a question about life and their future. For example, when asked if they believe they can be successful in starting a business and making money, they will say "YES!" in a heartbeat. Yet in their heart of hearts I have found far too many do not really believe that to be true at all.

It reminds me of being in conservative Christian churches when the pastor who has raised their voice and tenor to a near froth shouts to their flock, "Do you BELIEEEEVE that with God at your side you can do anything?!" Upon hearing this, the flock matches the question to what they have learned from Sunday school classes and elsewhere and upon doing so reacts with equal emotion saying, "YES! Praise God, YES!" Then the pastor may ask the question again to make sure and wake up any who were not paying attention or to get a louder response, "I said, DO YOU BELIEEEEVE THAT WITH GOD AT YOUR SIDE ANYTHING IS POSSIBLE?!" At that the flock now rises up as if one with hands lifted up shouting, "YES, SWEET JESUS I BELIEVE!" their hands waving in the air with a lot of Amens and Hallelujahs thrown in for added emphasis. Now cue in Alexandra Burke singing *Hallelujah* and the moment and mood would be perfect.

And though I am poking fun at this too familiar church routine, I will admit to believing if we discover the spirit of God within us, we actually *can* be who we were created to be and choose to a large degree where we will end up. However, the reality of most young people (and many adults) in and out of churches throughout the world today is *they do not believe it to be true* no matter how earnestly they shouted their belief when asked. They knew what to say when asked, yet deep within their heart of hearts they did not believe it. To them the circumstances they were born into will determine their future and nothing they will do will change that much. Their experiences and those of generations before have taught them well, and such mindsets are how they see the world and their life within it today including who to blame for their misery.

This is why after going to church or attending a workshop put on by a foundation, NGO, or even USAID, few have the capacity to sustain the excitement or knowledge the participants gained within the service or training. For the moment they walked out the door they left a world of safety and entered the twilight zone of the "real" world where everything around them was still the same, as were their lives. Some may hold on to their training or learning for a day, or a week or month but in time life goes back to the way it was and thus their need to return for another shot of hope from whatever source they can find it. This process itself can and has become an addiction for many in the world. There are exceptions to this of course but they are too few and far between.

This is why most trainings are not sustainable, for deep in their hearts those participating while shouting the belief and repeating the desired mantra or passing the final exams do not believe what is being said is true *for them*. And until that belief is changed, their lives and their realities will also remain virtually unchanged, and trainings will continue to fall woefully short in terms of the outcomes desired over time.

And while I am at it, it does not bode well for us to simply tell others what we believe they need to know. People learn by becoming engaged and through that engagement process their learning will come. It will not be us who will change those we are working with no matter how ardently we believe in the truth of our teachings. In the end it is only the people themselves that can change how they think and what they believe to be true. And for that to happen they must choose to be engaged. If anything, we are merely guides.

This is why after spending billions in Kenya by foreign governments, organizations and NGOs, the gap between the haves and have nots has not changed nearly as much as was intended. Our country alone is now spending over a billion dollars a year in aid to Kenya and that does not include any of the soft money coming into the country for health care, empowerment, job creation, and education!

As of 2013, half of the citizens of Kenya still live on less than 80 Kenyan shillings a day (1 USD). Corruption still permeates much of society in spite of thousands of new churches and people "saved." People still need to be empowered even though millions have been through empowerment trainings. Even job creation and economic development is still desperately needed in spite of millions of Kenyans having been trained in such things over the past 10 years or so.

How is it possible there are such huge gaps remaining today after years of empowerment, capacity building, entrepreneurship and leadership trainings to virtually millions? Clearly what is being done is not working yet the system continues doing the same things which of course is an accepted definition of insanity.

In fact, there have been many well-intentioned programs over the last few decades but instead of empowering, the unintended consequence has been to create a deep dependency on the money, the programs and the foreign aid process. It is so bad now that in Kenya the first questions many will ask when informed they are eligible to attend a training are, "How much will they pay? Will I get a transport fee and per diem? Will it be in a nice hotel and will they be providing food and tea?"

If the program does not pay much, many will choose not to attend. For those attending, they will be attending for the money and not for the learning and certainly not to change their lives in any deep or sincere way. Of course this is a broad brush painting everyone which of course is not fair. There are many who are working very hard to change things, just not nearly enough to carry the day.

As an example, Mary Okioma, the Kenya Law Society and I as a volunteer helper, did a workshop on the new constitution before the referendum. People attending were told in advance and when arriving there would be no money given as this was simply an information forum for those wishing to learn about what the potentially new constitution actually said. Some latecomers came expecting to be paid money and when told there was no money began to protest and make a lot of noise. At one point one screamed while pointing at us, "They have money to give us but are keeping it all for themselves and leaving us with nothing!" Things quickly spiraled out of control at that point as Mary and I and others were whisked away quickly just barely ahead of a mob of angry people demanding their money, which of course there was none.

This is why so many programs fail to sustain themselves or why, when groups of Kenyans are given money to start a business, the business fails soon after the money or funding is gone. In too many cases, those forming the group in the first place formed it because they heard there was money being given out. A portion of the group will work hard and be dedicated while the others will simply idle along or do only the bare minimum to remain in the group. Once the program is over, the majority who didn't really want to do or continue to do the project will demand that everything be sold and the money proceeds "shared" to each member of the group.

The end result: money to help empower, create jobs and grow the economic base ends up in the hands of people who will eventually spend it for food, school fees or worse alcohol, with few if any jobs created or sustained and no appreciable change occurring.

And what of the people, you ask? They are waiting for the next program, or loan or grant or training to come along with famine still an issue, poverty still an issue, drought still an issue, and unemployment still an issue with no end in sight.

And yet the process continues as the Foundations, NGOs, Government Ministries and agencies have provided their "donors" with all of the information and all the statistics of how many people were served or how many condoms or Bibles were distributed, churches built or people "saved." So the donors are happy in thinking they are making a difference thus continue to give, the NGOs and other entities are happy as money they need to survive is still coming in and the gaps to be closed and the reason for all of the aid programs in the first place continue to increase. The system is dysfunctional and broken and yet it continues as even they do not know how to think differently from what they already know.

There is a very good report done by the U.S. Congressional Research Service on Kenya throughout the years and its situation and challenges today. You will find the U.S. aid figures on page 15:

http://www.fas.org/sgp/crs/row/R42967.pdf

So it was with this in mind I wanted to help the women create their project but not without first working hard to change their mindsets, to slowly help them change how they think and behave from the standard reacting and repeating the behavior exhibited with other aid programs.

I wanted to help them to learn and choose to think differently. I wanted them to respond and create something new, something better rather than continuing to simply react and repeat their past. I wanted them to learn how and later actually choose to lead themselves from the inside out.

It was only by getting this accomplished would there be any chance of long-term success for the women in the group, their families and eventually all they would encounter within their communities and region. I knew if they would choose to understand, accept and deeply believe the concepts of responding and creating, they could change everything. But if they chose to think the same ways they had been taught and experienced, then nothing would change in the end and all would have been for naught.

So it is in that context I tried to find the way to help them create and sustain their dream which was the dairy herd but was in reality their dream of getting out of poverty and living a life of purpose and meaning.

But *how* to help them with no money of my own to give was the first challenge. I went back to taking a leap of faith. I once again put things out into the universe to see what might be attracted or come this way. It is one of the true gifts of social media today.

I wrote about the women, their experiences, their dream and their needs. I thought if I could get people to help buy three cows it would be enough to get them started. I was really naïve I will now admit for it would take much more than merely three cows. As to the challenge of changing their mindsets, well it looked good on paper but has been so very hard to do in the real world.

Helping people break away from the prison of what they think they know within their own minds to thinking differently is like trying to convince someone that jumping out of a perfectly good airplane with a sheet packed in a bag on one's back is the right thing to do. For those choosing to think differently or jump, they will experience the same thing: freefall. To some it's a rush they wish to experience again. To others it is a fright they never again wish to experience. Sadly for far too many, there is a stubborn refusal to think differently or to jump as they are OK with the way things are thank you very much!

Anyway, I put out the story of what I wished to do throughout social media and the donations came in. When the small donations of people literally throughout the world were counted there was enough for three cows, a water system for the primary school, fencing and a milking station. And with that what was once a dream had taken a step to becoming reality.

As the donations come in, a primary school's ruling committee (school board) near the women was so happy the women were not brewing anymore they decided to do something to help them succeed so they would not return to brewing. They also wanted to encourage and show other brewers if they quit brewing, help would come. So the committee gave the women permission for any cows they may receive to graze and be kept on the school's eight acres for three years at no cost. In return, the women's group used some of their funding to repair and build a new pump and water tank so that the 400 children of the school would have fresh water on their property rather than having to walk to the nearest river to bring back water in buckets to drink, wash clothes, cook and wash dishes. It was truly a win/win, not to mention healthier as water from the river can be very unhealthy for anyone using it as their primary source of water.

When the day finally came where the cows were going to be given to the women, the whole community came out in celebration. It was during that celebration where the Elders of the area gave me my Kalenjin name, Kiprotich. It means when the cows are coming home in the evening, and as it was late afternoon and the three cows were indeed coming "home," they felt that to be appropriate.

So I guess you can add that to your names now too if you wish! David Andrew and Matthew Thomas Rotich Bernard-Stevens! And though long, it would contain much about the history of your family and who you are. By the way, the reason your name would be Rotich and not Kiprotich is because Rotich stands for "son of Kiprotich" in the Kalenjin tradition.

All was well and everyone happy but reality soon came into clear focus for there were expenses the group had now for their new cows and the quantity of milk being produced by two of the three cows was woefully small. It was almost enough to cover most of the expenses for the cows but saving to eventually buy more cows or eventually buying the land they would need in three years was not possible. Many times the women had to dip into their own pockets to meet unexpected expenses and that put an increased strain on their already tight family budgets and small businesses.

And while most were working to expand their small business, not all were successful in doing that. Some because the scope of their business was too small, some because they were not willing to work harder, and others because their husbands would forcefully take their money earned for their own use – usually to drink away the profits on illegal alcohol still being brewed by other women not in the group. That irony was not lost on the women in the group; money from their hard work was sometimes going to other brewers doing what the group chose not to do in order to improve their lives.

It soon became clear to me that the stress of meeting the needs of the cows until more calves were born and milk production increased would be too much for many of the women. They simply did not have the capacity to meet those needs given the limited income they were receiving from their newly created small businesses. It was as if everyone heard the brewers talking and saying, "Look at you! The 14 of you have only three cows among all of you, you have to spend more of your money to get this dream of yours going and you still only have your small business to do it in. We may not be in a nice business but at least we have more money than you! You should sell the cows, share the money and come back to brewing!" It is amazing how many people do not want others to succeed and as such will do almost anything to bring them down. That is especially true in Kenya.

Those voices were loud with some outsiders stirring the pot at every turn. In time the women nearly split into two groups: one wishing to share the cows and just go back to the way it was, and the others who wanted to continue the journey believing that the income would come but not for five or more years... but they believed it would come.

In the end, the women found it within themselves to come together and reform around their original vision and dream. My sense is that once those who wished to go back to the way it was discovered the others were going to move forward, they quickly chose to say what was needed in order to remain in the group. For if they remained in the group and if there was indeed money to be had in the future, they did not want to be left out. So an agreement to move forward was reached although a deep commitment to do what needed to be done by all was still lacking in some. And, like the early Americans who compromised, allowing slavery to continue in the American Constitution in order to get a unanimous agreement, the issue of women not having a true commitment to the vision of the group would come back and bite them hard.

One thing producing a lot of stress for many of the women was many of their smaller children were now becoming old enough to attend high school. Now in 2015 Kenya, primary schools are free in terms of tuition although there are still many fees and expenses many parents cannot afford to pay. Secondary school, however, is another matter. They are not free and tuition fees can be high for a good school or relatively cheap for a bad one. For many of these women, stress was increasing as they could not see how they could afford keeping up with the dairy project, expand their own business and obtain the amount of funds to pay the upcoming school fees. Many considered going back to brewing and in fact four did, which meant they were no longer part of the women's group and dairy project.

The stress was taking its toll as the group shrank from the original courageous 16 down to the magnificent 11. Not all went back to brewing. One simply did not share the dream of having a dairy herd. I don't think she ever imagined the group would ever really have one so when it began to happen, she simply was not willing to dip into her pockets to support it. Perfectly understandable. She still has not gone back to brewing and is doing well with the small businesses she created while being with the group.

So in order to relieve the upcoming pressure I decided to ask people to help fund the school fees for those children in the group about to enter high school. The intention was to relieve the women's financial pressure to keep them moving forward in their project and businesses and not to go back to brewing. See what I mean about my being so incredibly naïve about three cows being all that was needed to get the group started?!

Once again people around the world were amazing in their financial support. The initial donations covered five children's school fees and three years after starting the program we were able to find the funds for 17 students as more of the group's children were becoming eligible for high school and at times there were funds remaining so that we could help other children who would otherwise be staying home.

I can't mention all who donated but I do want to tell you that many of the students I taught back at North Platte and Papillion/LaVista High Schools over 30 years ago stepped up and donated big time! It was a humbling experience to see their support and the fact they remembered me after all of the years brought a smile to my heart.

And that's how my "fundraising" began when I myself had nothing to give. I told the stories and people around the world responded. It has been an amazing and wonderful thing to be a part of. I have been constantly amazed at the capacity of people to give of their own hard-earned money to people in need they do not know, living in places they have never been. The generosity and capacity to love of the human spirit truly has no bounds when unleashed.

Over time the herd has grown from three to nine... and yes they have lost some cows along the way. The three years the school gave was extended to four but the time when the women would have to find their own land was fast approaching and failure to do so meant there would be no place for their cows.

Yet the milk production was still about four to five liters per day per producing cow. Not enough to buy land any decade soon but the women had begun finding ways to change how they handled their cows so that their four to five liter producing cows would produce 25 liters per cow per day in the future. It is called zero-based grazing and there are a few farmers in their locality who have been very successful at it so the women traveled to learn how to create their own facility when the time came.

So now the women knew the type of facility they needed and the feed necessary to increase their milk production and resulting revenue beyond anything they had imagined. But to do any of it they needed land and that was not within their capacity to do.

Once again people from around the world came through and after a short but grueling social media fundraising campaign called "Operation Dirt!" enough was raised for the women to purchase 1.9 acres of land. Now they had a place for their cows and if they worked hard and saved as much as possible, in time they would begin to build their own zero-grazing dairy facility of which they had all studied and learned how to create.

Since this process would increase the milk producing capacity of their cows from five to 15 to 25 liters per cow per day, many of the women were starting to do the math. They were beginning to see what their future could be perhaps in five to eight years if they continued to work hard and could avoid any devastating disasters. But there were still those who also saw the potential money but were not committed to do the work. This would continue to be a problem that would have to be dealt with at some point by the group.

They were also beginning to see the "asset" side of business. They were introduced to the concept of net worth and for the first time began to see the value of doing a business which was more than just spending what was earned for that day's work. This was a new concept to their thinking. In survival mode everything is done for money *now* and it is received and spent immediately. The wealthier in the world know the way to accumulate capital is to get their money to work for them. Now that concept was becoming more real within the mindsets of many of the women. Some were still reacting and wishing to sell everything and share, but now there was a majority who were responding to a new concept of what they could do each day to create a new future for their families.

Yet I will tell you they still have a long way to go in their learning to think differently. Each time I think real progress is being made, one or two of the group members do something that seems to take the group back to square one.

And now as I am writing you this I have received word that the group of 11 is now down to nine. Both of those being removed were from the group who did not have a real commitment to the vision. One was secretly brewing again and was caught and arrested by the police. The other had to be dropped for failing to do what was needed each month in terms of payments to the group.

Part of me is sad as I of course wanted magic to happen and all the women would find themselves out of poverty with lives of meaning and joy. But life isn't like that and the reality of the Kenyan saying is true: "You must remove the bad potatoes from the sack lest they spoil and destroy them all." By their choices the bad potatoes are removing themselves which in the end will help the rest succeed. But there is another saying that also comes to mind: "The only thing that is certain is that there is no certainty."

But the biggest factor still is their willingness to think differently when there is so much influence and pressure all around them not to. I feel they will succeed or fail in their dream-building on this point alone over time; their ability to think differently so they can create something new in their lives and of those around them. One thing is certain, there is no certainty.

As I have indicated before, I truly believe in the power of thought and action to attract similar things. The universe to me is a non-judgmental place such that if one puts out negative actions and thoughts, negative things will be attracted in an equal fashion in return. If positive thoughts and actions are put out into the universe, good things will be attracted. Perhaps this was what was meant in the ancient days when it was said by working, thinking and acting in the "right" way, God will always provide. I always thought the concept to be silly. I do not think so now.

I say this because of what the actions of these women have attracted. Initially they attracted a young man (Andrew) and later through him, me. Then their actions throughout all of their challenges attracted the help of people all over the planet, and now their work so far and their buying of 1.9 acres of land attracted an organization named IOM or International Organization for Migration. This organization believed in what these women had done and would continue to do thus choosing to fund their zero-based grazing facility. IOM was attracted to them by what the group had done by their actions.

As I type this, the women have completed construction of their facility and the cows have come to their new home. They are still years away from making positive cash flow, but the pieces of their initial dream are in place now just needing sustained effort, commitment and the ever important change of mindset and aligned action. The group is down to nine now and it is possible over time that there may be a further "weeding out." Yet the core group of eight will remain strong I believe and in the end it will be they who will change the lives of so many over time.

Perhaps here is as good a place as any to mention something that has bothered me about what I dreamed of doing here and its relationship to you, at least in my mind. Over the next few years my journey will no doubt put me into more circumstances where I may feel the need to help various groups and or people. Helping them will be truly my choice yet the *means* for that help will no doubt come from others around the world who believe enough in what I am doing to donate. This you know.

And yet I have never been able to shake the thought that here I have been in Africa helping people I didn't know and in fact doing little to nothing to help either of you. I sometimes struggle with the question, "Did

I abandon my responsibility as a father to my own children when I left for Africa?"

Now don't take this the wrong way, David, but during the time I left for Kenya, you had already married Sarah and had begun your own life and together building your own dreams. I don't feel quite so bad about not being able to help much during this time as you were already on your own with income etc. But you, Matt, were another story.

I remember the trip you and I made down to Florida to see if you would like it there knowing that you had support and a lifeline if needed from your Aunt Cris and Uncle Ron who lived nearby. Eventually you would choose to attend college there. But out-of-state tuitions were high, expenses too and I did nothing to help out in those areas. Your mother and her husband, Grandmother Joyce and Grandpa Jess, took over the necessary financial support when needed.

Still the question remains deep within me, "Did I choose to work hard to help others where I could have chosen to stay in the U.S., work hard to try to do my part as your father to help both you and David?" When I step back and look at my actions as if on a balcony overlooking the play of my life, I think the real answer to that is, yes, I think I did. I left your care in the hands of others as I went to build that which I believed (still do) was what I was meant to do with my life.

Was it a totally selfish act on my part? As I observe it from my make-believe balcony, I believe it was and yet I also think there comes a time when a person must choose to do what they were created to do or not. I now know that whenever that choice comes, it comes with a price as the leap of faith to be taken will jump one from the reality of what was into a new unknown reality where nothing is the same anymore.

When I try to find justifications, the elixir that takes one's pain away for a while, I have found three: one, that fortunately by their dedication, sacrifice and hard work, your mother and your Grandma Joyce and Grandpa Jess were very capable of giving you the financial help you would need; two, that as you, Matt, once said to me one day as we spoke briefly about this, "Heck Dad, you could give me all you had and it wouldn't help out much, no offense intended" and three, I knew the two of you would be fine and it was time for me to go where my own spirit was telling me I needed to go.

I guess when it is all said and done, if you think and feel that I abandoned you and selfishly went to do what I wanted to do with not a care for you, I ask for your forgiveness. In my mind that was not and still is not the case. I believe there are many ways a parent can be of help to their children. Perhaps mine is to show and to let you experience with me the joy and challenges of following your heart or spirit and that as individuals we are never trapped by life but merely by our own choices, which we have the power to change. And with that, even for both of you, building one's dream and doing what one believes one was meant to do is really only a choice away at any one moment in time.

But that is the reality from only my perspective I know. It is the one I wish to see. That plus the fact technology today has allowed us to stay in contact as often as we have chosen to do so.

And yet I remember when growing up, one of my dad's brothers, Uncle Sam, was always talked about by many in the family as "the black sheep of the family." Of course it meant that his choices were not those which fit their mindsets of what a responsible man should do. I suspect there are many within our extended family who now believe the same thing about me and the choices I have made.

And yet, having traveled this road less traveled, I have come to realize that it was Uncle Sam who was perhaps the one person within the family who was truly living life as it was meant to be lived. It is all according to the mindset one chooses to have I think. You will have to choose the mindset you wish to have to experience life. Just remember if ever you feel trapped, you are only a choice away from something new with a reality of meaning, purpose and joy.

Oh and as for Uncle Sam, he died of course about a year ago but he knew I had married a Kenyan woman and in true Uncle Sam form asked me how the "chicks of Kenya" were! He also sent 100 dollars to help what I was doing which for Sam at that time was a lot of money. For me it meant everything and in that his spirit still lives on.

My wish for the two of you is that you too find that inner peace and happiness in your lives as well.

Love to you both,
Dad

Talking with secondary students in rural Kenya on the concepts of learning how to think differently in order to create a new future.

June 23, 2014

Carrying water for building their zero-based grazing facility.

Lena's way of saying "we can and will do it!"

The Women's group saying "Thank You" for everyone who believed in them!

September 17, 2014

Dear David and Matt

I sense this will be my final letter to you in terms of my attempt to give you a sense of your father and a bit of my journey in life. Like you I have simply done the best I could with what I had within the circumstances that came my way. In the end it is all any of us can do to survive the lives we have been given with seemingly little choice.

I remember when I was young, your Grandmother DJ or Grandpa Dave (my father) would tell bedtime stories to my sisters Cris and Danna and me. Dad usually made his up on the fly with the best being about Gus and George – two balloons who had amazing adventures! Mom's stories were OK but they *always* had a moral to them on how we should act or behave. Hers were not nearly as fun as they always hit a little too close to home.

And yet I understand now what she was feeling. There is so much a parent wants to say to their children in order to help them avoid some of the pitfalls they experienced in their own lives.

There is so much I still want to say to you as well but in the end you will make your own choices and do your best to crawl out of the pitfalls you will discover or fall into as your lives unfold, just as you will shout for joy from the mountain tops you will master.

Yet I suppose it is true that in many ways I am like my mother as I cannot seem to resist stating some last thoughts.

We are our thoughts. What we see is through the mindsets we have built from all we have learned along the way. Those mindsets are how we interpret the world around us and as such, they tell us what we think is true or false whether it is or not. Unfortunately, based upon how much we do not know, those reactive decisions of determining truth are dubious at best.

I am not sure when I came to this realization, but it is very important for people to develop a process for self-reflection or meditation as we age. It is a way we can reconnect with our spirit. When I began to take time to reflect upon my own spirit, I was shocked as to the deep wisdom and knowledge it seemed to hold. Who knew?! Our spirits are truly amazing and something I suspect few will totally understand as the magnitude of its power and "knowing" will undoubtedly be greater than our time on earth to fathom it all. Perhaps that is what the phrase "God is unknowable" is all about. Even we will never totally know ourselves. It is a constant journey of discovery ending only when our time runs out. It also implies our need to continually explore new horizons and ideas in order to get the best understanding of ourselves.

From the moment of our birth and our journey's beginning we were all curious explorers. We became curious about everything and our capacity to ask "why" became the exasperation of many a parent. Watch any child and you will see their intense, almost instinctive desire to explore and learn. We seemed to have no fear of the unknown when young and an insatiable curiosity to know more.

Yet at some point along our journey we lose that curiosity as it is replaced with a newly discovered sense of fear stemming from our learning and experiences. We begin to fall into comfort zones satisfied or resigned to the way things are. From that point our true sense of who we are, those amazing explorers, begins to fade away until we no longer remember who we once were. Our journey from being close to our spirit at birth into being connected almost totally with our mind's "knowing" as we age becomes complete. Sadly, we are never the same after that and clearly there is less joy within the lives of far too many people.

That being said, my experience has been whenever I am going beyond my current reality and actually exploring new ideas and places I get a sense of excitement, passion and joy.

I should also warn you.

As you journey into what you do not know (many times by questioning what it is you know) you will run into intense feelings of fear, uncertainty and anxiety. They are also part of exploring the world of the unknown. If it helps, I have found when experiencing the intensity of the above emotions, it is then I feel alive and feel I am truly living the life my spirit was intended to live. I also sense this is true for most people if not everyone.

The book *The Dream Giver: Following Your God-Given Destiny* written by Bruce Wilkinson speaks so clearly about the fears we have when getting out of our comfort zone:

> **Ordinary saw his choice clearly now. He could either keep his comfort or his Dream. But how do you "take courage" when you don't have any?**
>
> **Ordinary decided. If his fear wasn't going to leave, he would have to go forward in spite of it.**
>
> **Still trembling, he picked up his suitcase, turned his back on Familiar, and walked to the sign. And even though his fear kept growing, Ordinary shut his**

eyes and took a big step forward – right through the invisible Wall of Fear.

And there he made a surprising discovery.

On the other side of that single step – the exact one Ordinary didn't think he could take – he found that he had broken through his Comfort Zone.

Now the Wall of Fear was behind him. He was free, and his Dream was ahead.

Joseph Campbell had a phrase that strikes me as also being appropriate here, "The cave you fear to enter holds the treasure you seek."

And yes, the more we learn, the more we realize how much more there is to know. Each step of obtaining new information, each passing along of that information to others, each journey into what is still unknown helps us create a better understanding of who we are, the universe we find ourselves in and the human spirit which is such an amazing and precious thing. When we overcome our fears and enter the caves of the unknown, we will find treasure and we will be the better for it.

Mahatma Gandhi is reported to have said that physical death is the birth of spiritual life. And though I believe that phrase to be true, I also believe we need not die physically to begin to grow our spiritual life.

Yet the concept of from death comes life is sound. For only when we choose to let our previous mindsets, thoughts and behaviors die can we find a rebirth of thought and spirit in our lives in any given moment. This is the heart of learning to think differently. At its core is a shift of being from becoming stuck within the prison of our mind into becoming responders and creators of our future (new life) as we reconnect our mind with our spirit to find the power and focus needed to get to the next level of who we were created to be.

And yet it is a choice. It is always a personal choice each of us at some point in our lives must make. Some choose to stay within the illusions they have created in their own minds rooted firmly in comfort zones. That is a perfectly understandable decision. Others choose to find treasure, growth and a better understanding of that which is surrounding them. They choose to be as they once were, explorers who find new lands, new ideas, new insights and better ways to lead both the self and with others to make a better world for all.

Whenever people choose to do those things, there comes a sense of excitement that simply cannot exist within our comfort zones. And all of us need to make that choice for along with that choice is the path and the power to change our lives into something more meaningful, full of energy, passion and best of all... joy!

From this viewpoint one begins to understand there is no such thing as some individuals being born leaders and others not. Everyone is born being both a leader (as we can all lead ourselves) *and* an explorer! It is only a matter of choice. When we reconnect with our spirit we find again the explorer within us which will lead us into the unknown, a brighter light and perhaps, enlightenment.

Along with this discovery comes the power to enter the once fearful cave to find the treasure of knowledge waiting patiently to be discovered. It is the information of who we are, what we need to do to be all we can be, and above all it is the knowledge we have the power within us to do exactly that. But we must look inward to find it.

When we lead from within, we become the leader we were created to be. Until we learn to lead ourselves from the inside out, we can never lead others. We can administer, manage and coerce others of course but we will never be able to lead.

Please know how much I love both of you and how very proud I am of you. I am honored to be able to call you my sons. I pray you make the kind of choices only you know deep down need to be made and that both of you live each moment of your lives with inner peace and joy... no matter how difficult the circumstances of your lives may become.

I also hope in time the two of you will find a way to become closer to each other. Your past can define your future relationship or you can create the one of your choice. You both have so much to offer each other. In time I know you will see that, hopefully sooner rather than later.

I never did ask the questions to know my father. In the end, the relationship we had chosen to create for ourselves was mended but there was not enough time for us to answer all of the questions we each had for the other. I pray these letters will make it so you will have some of the answers to the questions you wished you had asked me but never got around to.

As to what will happen in my life as I and my body continue to age to the protest of my mind and spirit, I have no idea as that chapter of my life's book has yet to be written. The possibilities are infinite and certainly not totally under my control. That being said, with Ruth at my side I know we will do our best to continue developing our shared dream of creating better leaders in the world who can create sustainable positive change.

I also know I have the power to control who I will become and to a large degree where I will be going. I also know whatever I think and do will have to mix in with all the other things happening in the universe I am in a relationship with and it will be from that mix of primordial brew the outcomes will emerge. And since you and I are all in a relationship of one sort or another with everything, the possibilities of what my future holds, and yours, are unlimited.

Even if we knew what the final results of our lives would be, the perceptions of it would be so different for everyone that no clear reality would ever emerge – except the one created within our own spirit and mind. And in the end, that is the one which will mean the most for us. So choose your realities wisely.

It is the same as stars being born within giant nebulas like the one near the sword of the mighty hunter comprising the constellation Orion. We are born from the essence of the creation of the universe and it is to that our energy and spirit will return in one fashion or another. What will be remembered will be what is interpreted in the future from the past and as such it will all be an illusion as anyone observing it will create their reality from their own perspectives and mindsets... which is why how people in the future remember us really doesn't matter.

The only thing that truly matters is whether we by our thoughts and actions choose to be all we were created to be to the best of our ability with the cards we were dealt with. If we do that, we will experience the joy, passion, commitment and purpose as a gift from the Universe (God) for the way we chose to "be."

I love you David. I love you Matt. God speed as you each choose the paths you will take to make a difference in the world. When you sense it is your time to take your own leap of faith, I hope you have the courage to take it. You will be amazed at what you will find and create. But watch that first step as it will be a doozy!

*Love, with respect and
with great gratitude, I am*

Your father,

*David Forsythe Kiprotich Bernard-Stevens,
born David Forsythe Stevens, III*

☺

Matt Bernard-Stevens.

Trying to make a difference in the world as best I can.

February 21, 2015

Acknowledgements

How does one say thank you to all of the people, known and unknown, who have by their thoughts, choices and actions pushed, guided, encouraged and otherwise influenced my getting to where I am now? And of course it is a fair question to ask where exactly that place is!

It is that place where I began doing what I was always meant to do. It is the place where my spirit is both at peace and on fire. It is the place where I found meaning and purpose in my life where joy is more often felt than not. It is the place where all human beings yearn to be... and can be.

I also wish to thank all who became frustrated with me, were harsh, mean-spirited and judgmental throughout my life as well. Without you I would not have been challenged to break through the barriers of frustration, despair, anger or doubt. Each of you was part of building who I eventually became and for that I sincerely thank you.

Of course I want to thank my sons David and Matt, my mother DJ and sisters Cris and Danna for all that they are and all they have done to impact my life one way or the other!

I also want to give recognition to some special people in my life: John Way, Mike and Susan Swanton, Roberta Brown Ellis, Dr. Mike Chipps, Mary Okioma, Jerry Wilson, Rhea D'Souza, Keith Blackledge (now deceased), Helen Okioma and Vicki Okumu. Thank you all for having the courage to be who you are and for picking me up when I needed help and especially bringing me out of the darkness and into the light when all seems too overwhelming. You will always be part of my life as you each live within my heart.

And as for you Ruth, words cannot describe the joy my life has had with you in it. I was truly blessed the moment your spirit ran into mine, we recognized each other and we became one.

And for the crew at Panoma Press… thank you. You became my guides, my mentors and my publishing "family." To Mindy, Emma, Alison and the entire crew, you have my deepest gratitude. May you bless others as much as you have blessed me.

David Bernard-Stevens

David is a political science graduate from the University of Nebraska with a teaching endorsement added in. He taught in public school systems within the United States (Nebraska) and has been an adjunct professor for Bellevue University and Mid-Plains Community College. He received his Master's Degree in Leadership from Bellevue University and later graduated from the international CTI Co-Active Leadership Program in California.

His interest in politics and the world came early as he studied at American University in Washington D.C. while working in the press liaison section of the United States Senate. It was a difficult time for the nation as international conflicts combined with the fight for civil and women's rights created much tension. It was here David began his true education about politics, world affairs, and leadership while learning from some of the best political minds of the times.

David reluctantly went into teaching young minds and to his surprise found great fulfillment and joy in helping others to think critically, broaden their perspective, and learn. He was chosen as Nebraska's Teacher of the Year in 1982 and was one of four national finalists for Teacher of the Year within the United States. Yet even with these honors, he sensed there was something more he should be doing and eventually gravitated into politics where he was a Senator in the Nebraska State Legislature for nine years. He never lost an election. From there he became President of a small Chamber of Commerce within the State of Nebraska.

Finding little fulfillment in Chamber work, David eventually formed his own business, Leader Development Group (LDG), as he felt the urge to go out into the world while combining his strengths as a teacher and knowledge of developing new authentic leaders. Soon afterward, he teamed up with Women for Justice in Africa to create and implement an empowerment and self-leadership program for women and youth throughout Kenya. From there, along with four brilliant Kenyans, he created a new Kenyan company, Effective Change Consultants Ltd where he currently serves as CEO.

While living and working in Nairobi, David continues to inspire people around the world to be the purposeful and ethical leaders they were born to be. He mentors clients around the world. His personal story of how he chose to take a "leap of faith" to totally change the direction of his life from business and politics to that of leadership development in the world is both powerful and inspiring.

Teaching in a way that allows individuals to personally grow, think differently and internalize concepts, David teaches the kind of leadership that will create growth and change others thought to be impossible. His teaching applies to businesses, corporate executives, organizations and individuals who want to build teams and programs that are resilient, sustainable and able to reach beyond the traditionally perceived boundaries. He is most happy, however, when inspiring people who have lost hope into discovering their own power to create their future from what they have with no need for a handout.

He gives people the critical thinking skills, tools, and knowledge so they may choose to be who they were created to be... and more. David and his team at Effective Change Consultants are currently delivering anti-corruption, ethical leadership and learning *how* to think differently trainings throughout Kenya and in time, the world.

In 2012, David married Ruth Jepngetich. David has two sons from a previous marriage, David and Matthew, who are both married and living in the United States.

Testimonials

"Real, raw and deeply inspiring! David's honest and vulnerable 'letters' are a brilliant doorway in to understanding our own humanity and the calling to our deeper sense of our own spirituality. He is a living example of 'faith made real.' Thank you David for sharing your life wisdom."

Rick Tamlyn -
Co-Founder, Bigger Game, Studio City, California

"The most enduring legacy we can leave may be those vulnerable moments when we struggle for the truth and ask questions with uncertain answers. This is what David Bernard-Stevens has gifted his sons with these letters. May you be inspired to create your own legacy of courage."

Jane Chin, Ph.D. -
MicroBusiness Strategy and STEM Leadership,
Medical Science Liaison Institute, Los Angeles, California

"It is an understatement to say that knowing David Bernard-Stevens and being asked to write a testimonial is a privilege. Knowing David transformed my life, and it fills me with joy to be able to recommend his writing to others. Through a happy set of "misfortunate" circumstances, I had the opportunity to participate in one of his early leadership workshops. I was going through a low period myself during that time – in fact, in one of the "lifeboat" exercises, I actually argued to be left to perish as everyone else in the group had more to offer humanity than I did. It wasn't an easy process, and it didn't end with the conclusion of the workshop, but I came to identify my true self and experience the beginnings of understanding the universe – the nature of the material world, the interconnectedness of everything, and most importantly, the "butterfly" effect.

"Though he is half a world away, David has continued to play a role in my life through his writings and Internet presence. His conversational writing style breaks down even the most complex concepts (Quantum Physics, anyone?) into easily understandable and applicable philosophies that truly make a difference. I encourage everyone to take "A Leap of Faith" and begin your own journey to self-revelation with David Bernard-Stevens."

Muriel Clark - *Sutherland, Nebraska*

"A Leap of Faith (who we are, where we are going and how to get there) is a phenomenal book. It will give hope to all of us in our disappointments and uncertainties that the world is still a good place to live, even with all its highs and lows especially within the hard moments of transformation. This book with its epistolary form directly appeals and invites us all to embark on an inward journey of self-discovery as humans and thereby unravel the world of others as well. It deserves to be a wonderful book for people to invest in since it would not only help people think differently but also create new possibilities and purpose - giving a new meaning to lives in the course of despair and depression, when they see no ray of light and darkness haunts and surrounds them. It would also teach and give all of us a magnificent inspiration to come out of our comfort zones in order to choose and discover a purposeful life.

Sadia Akram -
Government College University Faisalabad, Pakistan

"Many of us feel stuck, powerless to pull ourselves out of the 'prisons' we are living in. In this engaging book, A Leap of Faith, David Bernard-Stevens shows us how to think differently, discover who we are created to be, and make our dreams a reality. It is a journey everyone can take if we so choose."

Betsy Matsunaga - *Tokyo, Japan*

"Faith to believe in something you do not see – and the fruit of faith to see in that which you believe." David's life is a testimony to that many times over. I have known him for the past 10 years and have also had the privilege of working with him closely. I can say he has leaped… and fallen and got up again with his ability to laugh at himself and the circumstances.

"We are living in a world that is fragmented. Connections within families and ourselves are fractured and so too within society and will continue to remain that way. Our society has forgotten how to connect with each other and humanity and therefore continues to bleed.

"This letter from David to his two sons is a ray of sunshine on the "How" of this puzzle. And in that it uplifts the otherwise default future.

"A deeper experience of joy, as David puts it, is how his letter left me feeling. It's the kind of joy one feels amidst nature - truth - innocence and the sheer beauty of unapologetic authenticity.

"In our gender biased society, where men are condemned to "be men"- which is society speak for be strong, don't be vulnerable, don't show your feelings, be smart enough to circumvent your failures and lows, and of course don't tell all this to your grown-up sons.

"And yet that is exactly what David has done. Spoken from such an honest place in his heart which is both audacious and deeply heart warming at the same time. I can only imagine the courage it must have taken him to rummage through

memories and not be selective about them, and just pen it as it was, honest and with his characteristic humor.

"I am sure his sons will not just see him and the possibilities for themselves. In a world where putting on a mask has become an acceptable norm, for someone to write about his own authentic journey toward purpose and peace is like a fresh cool breeze that brings hope. I wish more people and especially fathers would take a page or two from David's book and reconnect, to themselves – their families and the futures of their spirit. This is the kind of book that one keeps going back to again and again. It's a journey in itself.

"There is hope. Thank you David... you have taken on Goliath." ☺

Rhea D'Souza -
Director - Paradigms Unlimited, Mumbai, India

"This book is an easy read. It makes one take time to reflect on their own life authenticity. It is a reminder of the importance of listening to our inner voice which always knows what our soul is longing for. The book demonstrates how things in one life could seem like they are falling apart only to direct us to our true calling/ purpose because if we continue with what does not work for our soul we will never experience the peace we experience by following our passion."

Love 'n' light

Motherk Masire -
Associate Director, Virtual World Enterprises, Gaborone, Botswana

"Leadership understood from its very beginning. A journey of leadership through self-mastery and a life in rural Kenya after serving a nine year term as a Nebraska state senator. A captivating read of a lifelong journey in leadership shared through letters to two grown sons living thousands of miles away from their father."

Vicki Okumu -
Founding Director, Effective Change Consultants, Nairobi, Kenya